MARTIN HEIDEGGER

'Timothy Clark's *Martin Heidegger* is an intelligent, highly accessible introduction to the German philosopher's complex intellectual trajectory. In its focus on Heidegger's engagement with art and language, Clark's book will be of particular interest to students of aesthetics, literature, and theory.'

Michael Eskin, *Columbia University*

'Heidegger was a uniquely gifted practitioner of the difficult art of reading. But his achievements have been overlooked or drastically misunderstood by mainstream literary theorists and critics. Timothy Clark's accessible, neat and reliable introduction goes a long way towards setting the record straight.'

Jonathan Ree, *Middlesex University*

Many critics consider Martin Heidegger the most influential, elusive and controversial figure in modern poetics and criticism. However, few students of literature have been directed to his writings on art and poetry. This volume offers such students a bridge to this crucial work.

Timothy Clark immerses readers in a new way of thinking, approaching Heideggerian ideas on the limits of 'theory' and of Western thought, his history of being, the origin and death of art, language, literature and poetics. He also covers the controversy of Heidegger's Nazi involvement.

Accessible and engaging throughout, this book will enable readers to take new critical approaches not only to literary texts, but also to the enduring traditions of Western thought.

Timothy Clark is a specialist in Romantic and post-Romantic poetics, based at Durham University. He is co-editor of the *Oxford Literary Review* and author of *Derrida, Heidegger, Blanchot: Sources of Derrida's Notion and Practice of Literature* (1992) and *The Theory of Inspiration* (2000).

ROUTLEDGE CRITICAL THINKERS
essential guides for literary studies

Series Editor: Robert Eaglestone, Royal Holloway, University of London

Routledge Critical Thinkers is a series of accessible introductions to key figures in contemporary critical thought.

With a unique focus on historical and intellectual contexts, each volume examines a key theorist's:

- significance
- motivation
- key ideas and their sources
- impact on other thinkers

Concluding with extensively annotated guides to further reading, *Routledge Critical Thinkers* are the literature student's passport to today's most exciting critical thought.

Already available:
Martin Heidegger by Timothy Clark
Gilles Deleuze by Claire Colebrook
Fredric Jameson by Adam Roberts
Jean Baudrillard by Richard J. Lane
Paul de Man by Martin McQuillan
Sigmund Freud by Pamela Thurschwell
Edward Said by Bill Ashcroft and Pal Ahluwalia
Maurice Blanchot by Ullrich Haase and William Large

Forthcoming:
Judith Butler

For further details on this series, see www.literature.routledge.com/rct

MARTIN HEIDEGGER

Timothy Clark

London and New York

First published 2002
by Routledge
11 New Fetter Lane, London EC4P 4EE

Simultaneously published in the USA and Canada
by Routledge
29 West 35th Street, New York, NY 10001

Routledge is an imprint of the Taylor & Francis Group

© 2002 Timothy Clark

Typeset in Perpetua by Florence Production Ltd, Stoodleigh, Devon
Printed and bound in Great Britain by TJ International Ltd,
Padstow, Cornwall

British Library Cataloguing in Publication Data
A catalogue record for this book is available from the British Library

Library of Congress Cataloging in Publication Data
Clark, Timothy, 1958–
    Martin Heidegger / Timothy Clark.
      p. cm. – (Routledge critical thinkers)
    Includes bibliographical references (p.) and index.
      1. Heidegger, Martin, 1889–1976. I. Title. II Series.

    B3279.H49 C53 2002
    193–dc21

                                                    200131919

    ISBN 0–415–22928–6 (hbk)
    ISBN 0–415–22929–4 (pbk)

For Kitty

'One can learn to ski only on the slopes and for the slopes'
(Heidegger)

CONTENTS

SERIES EDITOR'S PREFACE

The books in this series offer introductions to major critical thinkers who have influenced literary studies and the humanities. The *Routledge Critical Thinkers* series provides the books you can turn to first when a new name or concept appears in your studies.

Each book will equip you to approach a key thinker's original texts by explaining her or his key ideas, putting them into context and, perhaps most importantly, showing you why this thinker is considered to be significant. The emphasis is on concise, clearly written guides which do not presuppose a specialist knowledge. Although the focus is on particular figures, the series stresses that no critical thinker ever existed in a vacuum but, instead, emerged from a broader intellectual, cultural and social history. Finally, these books will act as a bridge between you and the thinker's original texts: not replacing them but rather complementing what she or he wrote.

These books are necessary for a number of reasons. In his 1997 autobiography, *Not Entitled*, the literary critic Frank Kermode wrote of a time in the 1960s:

> On beautiful summer lawns, young people lay together all night, recovering from their daytime exertions and listening to a troupe of Balinese musicians. Under their blankets or their sleeping bags, they would chat drowsily about the gurus of the time. . . . What they repeated was largely hearsay; hence my

lunchtime suggestion, quite impromptu, for a series of short, very cheap books
offering authoritative but intelligible introductions to such figures.

There is still a need for 'authoritative and intelligible introductions'.
But this series reflects a different world from the 1960s. New thinkers
have emerged and the reputations of others have risen and fallen, as
new research has developed. New methodologies and challenging ideas
have spread through the arts and humanities. The study of literature is
no longer – if it ever was – simply the study and evaluation of poems,
novels and plays. It is also the study of the ideas, issues, and difficulties
which arise in any literary text and in its interpretation. Other arts and
humanities subjects have changed in analogous ways.

With these changes, new problems have emerged. The ideas and
issues behind these radical changes in the humanities are often presented
without reference to wider contexts or as theories which you can simply
'add on' to the texts you read. Certainly, there's nothing wrong with
picking out selected ideas or using what comes to hand – indeed, some
thinkers have argued that this is, in fact, all we can do. However, it
is sometimes forgotten that each new idea comes from the pattern and
development of somebody's thought and it is important to study the
range and context of their ideas. Against theories 'floating in space',
the *Routledge Critical Thinkers* series places key thinkers and their ideas
firmly back in their contexts.

More than this, these books reflect the need to go back to the
thinker's own texts and ideas. Every interpretation of an idea, even the
most seemingly innocent one, offers its own 'spin', implicitly or
explicitly. To read only books on a thinker, rather than texts by that
thinker, is to deny yourself a chance of making up your own mind.
Sometimes what makes a significant figure's work hard to approach
is not so much its style or content as the feeling of not knowing where
to start. The purpose of these books is to give you a 'way in' by offering an accessible overview of a these thinkers' ideas and works and
by guiding your further reading, starting with each thinker's own
texts. To use a metaphor from the philosopher Ludwig Wittgenstein
(1889–1951), these books are ladders, to be thrown away after you have
climbed to the next level. Not only, then, do they equip you to approach
new ideas, but also they empower you, by leading you back to a theorist's own texts and encouraging you to develop your own informed
opinions.

Finally, these books are necessary because, just as intellectual needs have changed, the education systems around the world – the contexts in which introductory books are usually read – have changed radically, too. What was suitable for the minority higher education system of the 1960s is not suitable for the larger, wider, more diverse, high technology education systems of the twenty-first century. These changes call not just for new, up-to-date, introductions but new methods of presentation. The presentational aspects of *Routledge Critical Thinkers* have been developed with today's students in mind.

Each book in the series has a similar structure. They begin with a section offering an overview of the life and ideas of each thinker and explain why she or he is important. The central section of each book discusses the thinker's key ideas, their context, evolution and reception. Each book concludes with a survey of the thinker's impact, outlining how their ideas have been taken up and developed by others. In addition, there is a detailed final section suggesting and describing books for further reading. This is not a 'tacked-on' section but an integral part of each volume. In the first part of this section you will find brief descriptions of the thinker's key works: following this, information on the most useful critical works and, in some cases, on relevant websites. This section will guide you in your reading, enabling you to follow your interests and develop your own projects. Throughout each book, references are given in what is known as the Harvard system (the author and the date of a works cited are given in the text and you can look up the full details in the bibliography at the back). This offers a lot of information in very little space. The books also explain technical terms and use boxes to describe events or ideas in more detail, away from the main emphasis of the discussion. Boxes are also used at times to highlight definitions of terms frequently used or coined by a thinker. In this way, the boxes serve as a kind of glossary, easily identified when flicking through the book.

The thinkers in the series are 'critical' for three reasons. First, they are examined in the light of subjects which involve criticism: principally literary studies or English and cultural studies, but also other disciplines which rely on the criticism of books, ideas, theories and unquestioned assumptions. Second, they are critical because studying their work will provide you with a 'tool kit' for your own informed critical reading and thought, which will make you critical. Third, these thinkers are critical because they are crucially important: they deal with ideas and questions which can overturn conventional understandings of the world, of texts, of everything we take for granted, leaving us with a deeper understanding of what we already knew and with new ideas.

No introduction can tell you everything. However, by offering a way into critical thinking, this series hopes to begin to engage you in an activity which is productive, constructive and potentially life-changing.

ABBREVIATIONS

TEXTS BY HEIDEGGER

GA   *Gesamtausgabe* [*Collected Works*] Frankfurt: Klosterman, 1975– .

BP   *The Basic Problems of Phenomenology*, trans. Albert Hofstadter, rev. ed., Bloomington: Indiana University Press, 1982.

BT   *Being and Time*, trans. John Macquarrie and Edward Robinson, Oxford: Basil Blackwell, 1980.

C   *Contributions to Philosophy (From Enowning)*, trans. Parvis Emad and Kenneth Maly, Bloomington: Indiana University Press, 1999.

D   *Discourse on Thinking*, trans. John M. Anderson and E. Hans Freund, New York, NY: Harper & Row, 1966.

E   *Elucidations of Hölderlin's Poetry*, trans. Keith Hoeller, New York: Humanity Books, 2000.

EP   *The End of Philosophy*, trans. Joan Stambaugh, London: Souvenir Press, 1975.

H   *History of the Concept of Time: Prolegomena*, trans. Theodore Kisiel, Bloomington: Indiana University Press, 1992.

Heb   'Hebel – Friend of the House', trans. Bruce V. Foltz and Michael Heim, *Contemporary German Philosophy* 3 (1983), pp. 89–101.

Her.   (with Eugen Fink) *Heraclitus Seminars*, trans. Charles H. Seibert, Evanston, Ill.: Northwestern University Press, 1993.

HK   'Der Herkunft der Kunst und Die Bestimmung des Denkens', in *Distanz und Nähe: Reflexionen und Analysen zur Kunst der Gegenwart*, eds Petra Jaeger and Rudolf Lüthe, Würzburg: Königshausen und Neumann, 1983, pp. 11–22.

IM   *Introduction to Metaphysics*, trans. Gregory Fried and Richard Polt, New Haven: Yale University Press, 2000.

Ist.   *Hölderlin's Hymn 'The Ister'*, trans. William McNeill and Julia Davis, Bloomington: Indiana University Press, 1996.

Log.   'Logos (Heraclitus, Fragment B 50)', *Early Greek Thinking*, trans. David Farrell Krell and Frank A. Capuzzi, New York, NY.: Harper & Row, 1975, pp. 59–78.

Only   'Only a God Can Save Us', in Richard Wolin ed., *The Heidegger Controversy: A Critical Reader,* Cambridge Massachusetts: MIT, 1993, pp. 91–116.

N   *Nietzsche*, 4 vols., trans. David Farrell Krell, and (vol. 4) Frank A. Capuzzi, New York: Harper & Row, 1979–82.

P   *Pathmarks*, trans. Frank A. Capuzzi *et al.*, ed. William McNeill, Cambridge: Cambridge University Press, 1998.

Par.   *Parmenides*, trans. André Schuwer and Richard Rojcewicz, Bloomington: Indiana University Press, 1992.

PLT   *Poetry, Language, Thought*, trans. Albert Hofstadter, New York, NY: Harper & Row, 1971.

PR   *The Principle of Reason*, trans. Reginald Lilly, Bloomington: Indiana University Press, 1996.

QCT   *The Question Concerning Technology and Other Essays*, trans. William Lovitt, New York, NY, Harper & Row, 1977.

Rec.   'The Rectorate 1933/34: Facts and Thoughts', trans. Karsten Harries, *Review of Metaphysics* 38 (1985), pp. 479–502.

Self   'The Self-Assertion of the German University', trans. William S. Lewis, in Wolin ed., *The Heidegger Controversy: A Critical Reader*, pp. 29–39.

TB   *On Time and Being*, trans. Joan Stambaugh, New York, NY: Harper and Row, 1972.

U   *Überlieferte Sprache und Technische Sprache*, Switzerland: Erker Verlag, 1989.

WL   *On the Way to Language,* trans. Peter D. Hertz, San Francisco, Ca.: Harper & Row, 1971.

WT   *What is Called Thinking*, trans. J. Glenn Gray, New York, NY: Harper & Row, 1968.

OTHER TEXT

Pet. Heinrich Wiegand Petzet, *Encounters and Dialogues with Martin Heidegger 1929–1976*, trans. Parvis Emad and Kenneth Maly, Chicago: University of Chicago Press, 1993.

WHY HEIDEGGER?

Martin Heidegger is the hidden master of modern thought. His influence on thinkers in the second half of the twentieth century, though often unspoken, is all pervasive, especially in that mélange in the humanities known curiously as 'theory'. Heidegger's work touches the deepest, usually unconsidered assumptions of all work of thought, forming a reassessment of the drive to knowledge itself. In the second half of the twentieth century it was often under Heidegger's direct or indirect influence that the traditional view that intellectual and scientific inquiry, the search for truth, is inherently disinterested, or even critical of unwarranted forms of authority, gave way to arguments that the drive to know is often compromised by elements of domination and control. Heidegger died in 1976 at the age of eighty-six, and his work has become even more prominent since that time, especially in continental Europe where the decline of Marxism has brought Heidegger's radical critique of Western thought to a new prominence.

Heidegger's thinking concerns things so fundamental that those coming to Heidegger for the first time should be warned that the bases of just about everything they think, assume, or take for granted are at stake in his texts. Imagine that the whole of Western thought, since the time of the first philosophers in ancient Greece, has been in the grip of a prejudice affecting all its aspects and even what seems self-evident. This is something so deep and all-pervasive that it should not even be called a prejudice if that word implies choice and individual misjudgement rather than an unavoidable heritage into which people are born and receive their most seemingly immediate sense of themselves. This is Heidegger's massive claim, and his view of 'Western metaphysics' as being constituted in terms that call for 'deconstruction' has since become amplified in the work of the contemporary French thinker Jacques Derrida (1930–).

Heidegger's thinking is both a profound philosophy and a radical critique of the fundamental assumptions of modernity, understanding 'modernity' with the critic Lawrence E. Cahoone as:

> The positive self-image modern Western culture has often given to itself, a picture born in the eighteenth-century Enlightenment ... of a civilization founded on scientific knowledge of the world and rational knowledge of value, which places the highest premium on individual human life and freedom, and believes that such freedom and rationality will lead to social progress through virtuous self-controlled work, creating a better material, political and intellectual life for all.
>
> (Cahoone 1996: 12)

Heidegger is deeply reactionary in the proper, not necessarily condemning sense of the word. His thinking aligns him with those who 'see modernity instead as a movement of ethnic and class domination, European imperialism, anthropocentrism, the destruction of nature, the dissolution of community and tradition, the rise of alienation, the death of individuality in bureaucracy' (ibid). Although the term post-dates him, Heidegger is also a major thinker of 'globalization'.

Heidegger was a philosopher who gave supreme importance to some poetic texts. He retained, however, a philosopher's contempt for the field of literary criticism, with its mix of moralism and amateur philosophizing. If the literary takes on a new importance for Heidegger, it is because his thinking also disputes what 'philosophy' has always meant since classical Greece. In Reiner Schürmann's words:

> The responsibility traditionally incumbent on the philosopher, his true mission, consisted in securing ultimate referents or principles. Whether he analyzed substance and its attributes or consciousness and its intentional acts, he spoke as the expert on deep anchorage: an anchorage that guaranteed meaning in

discourse, soundness of mind, objectivity of knowledge, value of life, if not possible redemption from infractions.

(Schürmann 1990 : 286)

Heidegger pulls up the anchor. Against the aggressive drive of human reason to justify and understand human existence by reference to its authority alone, Heidegger insists on the limits and fragility of human knowledge.

Pervading all of Heidegger's work is an intense sense of crisis, of living at a grimly decisive time for the future of humanity. This sense grew initially out of the collapse and humiliation of Germany after its defeat in The First World War. Heidegger's response was one shared by many Germans at the time, a sense of the utter bankruptcy of the old civilized values and modes of life. Hans Georg Gadamer (1900–), who was to become Heidegger's most famous student, remembers the immense shock of first encountering Heidegger's teaching in the 1920s:

A generation shattered by the collapse of an epoch wanted to begin completely anew; it did not want to retain anything that had formerly been held valid. Even in the intensification of the German language that took place in its concepts, Heidegger's thought seemed to defy any comparison with what philosophy had previously meant.

(Gadamer 1994: 69)

Heidegger's thinking embraced not just the philosophical and social crisis of Germany at this time, but became a powerful reassessment of the most basic values and assumptions of Western civilization since ancient Greece. Gadamer describes the massive impact of Heidegger in lectures which encompassed ancient Greek thought and contemporary issues within the same powerful over-view: 'It was like a new breakthrough into the unknown that posed something radically new as compared with all the movements and countermovements of the Christian Occident' (Gadamer 1994, 69). While other thinkers of crisis from this time, such as Oswald Spengler and his once famous *The Decline of the West* (1918), have become of merely historical interest, Heidegger's thought retains an impact which is still working itself out.

Many intellectual positions often labelled 'postmodern' inhabit the space opened up by Heidegger's attacks on the absolutism of modernity's drive to know. Heidegger's effect has been to release a sense of the fragility of the grounds of human thought, art and culture generally, an effect reinforced by the influence of Heidegger's most famous contemporary follower, Jacques Derrida. It is ironic therefore that neither would endorse the relativism associated with the slogan 'postmodern' to the extent of abandoning the claims of truth and objectivity, by arguing, for example, that modern physics is no more valid or invalid than ancient Chinese astronomy, or that philosophy, science and religion all need to be thus 'relativized' as 'cultural constructs' (see Derrida 1999: 77–9; Polt 1999: 71–2, 103–6). Both are concerned to take received modes of philosophizing and thought to their limits, yet not with a view to merely discrediting or making them all on a level, but to trace the deepest assumptions of Western thought, its margins and boundaries, opening themselves in the process to what other modes of being and thinking, if any, might be conceived beyond it.

It is in this context that Heidegger turned to the poetic, not merely as one cultural discourse among others, or as an arena for competing historical forces, but as a singular mode of 'truth' and 'knowledge', meaning these no longer in the sense these have in philosophy or science traditionally understood, but precisely as modes of thought closed off and repressed by the Western tradition.

It is customary in a brief introduction like this to cover the biography of the thinker at issue. This is an approach Heidegger himself despised as a way of evading the one thing that matters in any thinker, the life of their thought. In any case, except for one issue, Heidegger's biography is pedestrian reading. He was born of a provincial Catholic family in Messkirch, in Swabia, Southern Germany in 1889. He turned from being trained as a cleric to the sciences and mathematics and then to philosophy, becoming the star pupil and then main follower of Edmund Husserl (1859–1938), founder of the school known as 'phenomenology'. Heidegger's magnum opus, *Being and Time* (1927), on which his reputation was largely based, is dedicated to Husserl, whose thought it none the less drastically undercuts. Heidegger became Husserl's successor, living the uneventful, slightly self-enclosed life of a professor of philosophy at Freiburg. He never left his native area of Germany, to which he felt deeply attached. He was buried in his home town in 1976.

The one exception to this uneventful story threatens to remain better known than anything of Heidegger's thought itself. In 1933, a few months after it had come to power in Germany, Heidegger joined the Nazi party. From 1933 to 1934 he gave the Nazis his support as Rector of Freiburg University. The extent of Heidegger's involvement is controversial, and it seems that some sort of disillusion set in swiftly from 1934. It was sufficient, however, for him to be banned from teaching for five years after the end of the Second World War. So readers of Heidegger have had to hold in their minds two almost irreconcilable facts. That Heidegger is widely regarded as the greatest philosopher of the twentieth century: that, for an uncertain time, he was a supporter of the Nazis. These issues are visited in Chapter 7.

CONTEXT

The template for the Routledge Critical Thinkers Series, imposed on every study within it, promises to put these crucial thinkers 'back' into their historical context. This is no doubt mainly an appeal to a current intellectual cliché with the aim of attracting readers. It raises, nevertheless, a vital question: what *is* the 'context' for a thinker like Heidegger, and what would it mean, assuming it were possible, to put him 'back' into it (as if he were some sort of escaped rabbit)?

The problem here is easily stated: a reading or argument by Heidegger, his work on the poet Rainer Maira Rilke (1875–1926) for instance (PLT: 91–142), will often find that understanding a specific term or issue means unravelling modes of thought that may have first been formed more than two millennia before (with the ancient thinker Parmenides in this case). Gadamer writes of Heidegger as having 'the determination of a thinker who saw the present and the past, the future and the Greeks as a totality' (Gadamer 1994, 114). So when Heidegger opens up Rilke's poetry with a view to ancient assumptions about humanity and being that still encompass the modern West, the 'context' at issue is not a 'historical' one in the normal, comfortable sense (as for a conventional critic who would open up the text by way of the context of Rilke's life, his politics, his social prejudices, religious debates and so on). Heidegger's is, at the very least, a context which modern people still inhabit – or which rather inhabits us to the extent that we will never be able to see it whole. The aim of putting Heidegger 'back' into his 'context' in that sense is thus incoherent, nonsensical. 'When people claim to be "against" Heidegger – or even "for" him – then they make fools of themselves. One cannot circumvent thinking so easily' (Gadamer 1994: 112).

Heidegger's refusal to be historicized in this containing way is the reason why his thought continues to impact and to be reread. Yet it is also the reason why the major feature of Heidegger's own immediate 'context', his engagement with the Nazis in the early 1930s, becomes so imponderable and disturbing (see Chapter 7). Of all the questions Heidegger's Nazi episode raises perhaps the most difficult is this one: how far may fascism also be integral to the broad context that the West still inhabits, but which it does not see?

This book is primarily an introduction to Heidegger for students of literature. Heidegger was a philosopher of many sides, but this book is about his thinking on questions of literature and criticism. Although there are several accessible introductions to Heidegger, focused on *Being and Time* (1927), this the first such work on Heidegger's poetics and literary theory, which almost entirely postdate that work. The first two chapters will focus on the crucial elements of the earlier Heidegger that continued into his turn to art and poetry in the mid-1930s. Chapters 3 and 4 are devoted almost entirely to Heidegger's great lecture. 'The Origin of the Work of Art', delivered in the mid-1930s and published in 1950. Chapter 5 looks at Heidegger's profound and counter-intuitive thinking about language, and Heidegger's own experiments with writing in dialogue form and his other experiments with different ways of writing in philosophy. This chapter also studies in some detail the kind of close reading Heidegger gives to a traditional philosophical text, in this case just one crucial term from the ancient Greek thinker Heraclitus. Attention to how Heidegger reads prepares the ground for understanding his distinctive approach to poetic texts, the detailed concern of Chapter 6. Here the focus turns to the significance Heidegger grants one extraordinary writer, the German romantic poet Friedrich Hölderlin (1770–1843). The second half of this chapter takes the reader through the main moves of Heidegger's reading of Hölderlin's ode 'Germania'. Chapter 7 concerns the scandal of Heidegger's involvement with the Nazis in the mid-1930s, and the fraught question of how this must affect the reception of his thought. Is it possible to answer claims that Heidegger's thinking remains essentially fascist or that it is merely reactionary in the narrow sense? Finally, a last chapter surveys Heidegger's all-pervasive if often unspoken influence upon literary study since the 1940s, especially his legacy in relation to the continuing 'deconstruction' of Western thought engaged by Derrida and others.

Heidegger's influence has been massive and incalculable on questions of poetic language, the nature of interpretation, the place of art and the crisis endured by the modern artist. However, the inaccessible and recalcitrant mode of Heidegger's writings makes any attempt to relate Heidegger clearly but also nonreductively to literary and critical debate a considerable labour of re-description and elucidation. So, even if it did not wish to be so, this book cannot but be original in the elucidations and redeployments it makes.

Heidegger's complete works are still being edited and translated. His greatest work on poetics, the influential study of Hölderlin, only appeared in English while this book was being written, a full fifty years late. New texts in the *Complete Works* appear each year and the tracing of Heidegger's paths continually involves new maps. So, this introduction also offers a response to the emerging implications and surprises of an extraordinary body of thought that is still appearing.

1

THE LIMITS OF THE THEORETICAL

It requires a very unusual mind to undertake the analysis of the obvious.

(A. N. Whitehead)

Heidegger is often acknowledged as the most decisive and most influential thinker of the second half of the twentieth century. All the same it is not hard to see why no introduction to Heideggerian poetics exists. Many assumptions usually at work in an introductory volume of this kind are exactly those Heidegger spent his lifetime attacking – the assumption that philosophical thought or literary reading are a matter of 'having a theory' and then putting it into practice, that there are 'key ideas' in the sense of conceptual packages that can be transferred like so many commodities across a counter, that a work of thought is in the business of making its matter available in the 'quickest and cheapest way' (D: 45). Heidegger's injunction to free ourselves from 'the technical interpretation of thinking' whose origins 'reach back to Plato and Aristotle' (P: 240) includes the notion that thinking is a kind of inner tool kit, containing 'ideas' to be picked up and employed on 'problems' as occasion requires. An introduction to Heidegger's thinking that does not at once register these issues has already failed to give a sense of its challenge and fundamental disturbance.

Nevertheless, Heidegger need not be hard to understand, once one accepts that he is questioning what 'understanding' or 'knowing' usually mean. Heidegger's topic is in fact the obvious, things so basic as to seem beyond question and self-evident. Heidegger's claim is that the course of European and increasingly global history has been largely determined as the hitherto unseen working out of utterly basic but usually unconsidered modes of thinking and being, dating back to ancient Greece. These are now culminating in a global techno-scientific civilization that Heidegger saw as a threat not just to the earth itself but to the essence of humanity, for such a 'civilization' is perfectly capable of regarding people as merely another economic resource or even a waste product. Freedom from this monolith is the concern of Heidegger's thinking. His books, said Heidegger, 'have only a single task, namely to let the being that we ourselves are become a real distress and a real liberation' (Pet: 100).

The issue is 'being', a concept dismissed by some philosophers as an empty abstraction, or the broadest generalization possible, for the least that one can say of anything, is that it 'is'. For Heidegger, it is neither pointlessly empty nor vacuously general: it is the neglected issue of Western thought, secretly determining its possibilities and its destructiveness. 'Do we in our time have an answer to the question of what we really mean by the word 'being'? Not at all' (BT: 19). Yet any time we think or speak of any entity at all, from a galaxy to a poetic text, we are already working, albeit unconsciously, within a set of assumptions about what is meant merely by saying of something that it 'is'.

Heidegger's 'history of being' can conveniently be thought of as a *history of the obvious*, which means not an obvious history but an attention to how the very horizon within which all things are unconcealed for us has changed, is itself historical. The surprising fact is that the obvious has a history and so becomes, as we read Heidegger, newly questionable. For a certain understanding of being has come, unnoticed but all pervading, to attune all of Western thinking and also 'common sense'. Heidegger names this 'the determination of being as presence'.

The 'determination of being as presence' is a lot to swallow at once. However, a basic point can be made quite briefly. Western thought, since the inception of philosophical questioning in ancient Athens, is driven towards a knowledge that would be a timeless unconditioned truth about the universe and human life, a knowledge based not on dogma, religious or otherwise, but on what is attested to human reason alone. The 'determination of being as presence' names, crudely speaking, the kind of thing that the world must be taken to be in order for it to correspond to and justify such an ideal of theoretical knowledge, a knowledge disengaged from its object and positing it neutrally, from the outside as it were. Such a stance on things, on being, interrogates them with a view to what can be construed as universally true, perpetually extant/present as an object of contemplation for the intellect. This is the supposedly 'true' world, perceivable with difficulty by the mind alone, as opposed the 'lesser' immediate world of sensations, passions and interests in which we find ourselves. For Heidegger, this whole two and a half millennia project of metaphysics and science needs to be drastically qualified. This is not in order to affirm some crass and vaguely 'postmodern' notion that all knowledge is 'merely relative', but to reawaken a fundamental questioning into the conditions, sources and limits of human knowledge. Here is just one issue to begin with. The drive to attain some realm of unchanging essential truths beneath phenomena is also, necessarily, the positing of human reason as the capable bearer of such a timeless stance. Is this, Heidegger would ask, a denial of our mortality, and of the historical nature of our existence?

METAPHYSICS

Metaphysics is traditionally the field of philosophy which asks the most fundamental questions about what things are. By 'fundamental' here is meant not just questions of the empirical kind that could in principle be resolved by experiment (such as that of the ultimate composition of matter, or the energy content of the universe) but questions which would remain even after all such issues were answered. Metaphysical questions would be: 'what is the nature of number?'; 'what is the distinction between the material and the non-material?'; 'what is cause and effect?'; 'why is there anything at all rather than nothing?' and, finally, 'what do we mean anyway when we say of something that it "is" or ask "what is . . .?"?'.

In Heidegger the term 'metaphysics' usually bears a negative inflection. 'Metaphysical' are those deepest, inherited decisions about what things are within which Western people immediately live. These are all-pervading, finding their most explicit expression in philosophers' writings on 'metaphysics' in the generic sense. In other words, Western humanity has lived within a certain understanding of fundamental questions since the ancient Greeks, assumptions it is now urgent to question.

Heidegger's is a thinking of the finitude of human life. Thought cannot transcend its own historicity, or achieve, except in fantasy, that kind of assured un-worlded 'truth' idealized in Western cultures. Yet Western life since the Greeks seems determined as a denial of this finitude, in a drive towards theoretical knowledge that is now culminating in the globalization of techno-science and bureaucratically mapped and controlled forms of life. This drive would culminate, or self-destruct, writes Heidegger, when human rationality comes to build up a theoretic representation of its own working so seemingly assured as to enable it to build its apparent duplicate. 'Sometimes it seems as if modern humanity is rushing headlong toward this goal of *producing itself technologically*' (P: 197). This is a 'nihilism', the drive that human thinking, impossibly or emptily, justifies itself with reference only to its own procedures, resting on 'values' only of its own positing. 'If humanity achieves this, it will have exploded itself . . .' (ibid). In directing his life's work against nihilism, Heidegger's thinking attempts to uncover a more fundamental, pre-reflective non-appropriative relation to being. This he saw at work in the kind of knowledge of things shown by traditional craftsmen, such as in a carpenter's deep, non-theoretical understanding of wood, or in the life of peasants or finally, to a degree, in art and poetry.

To make a start, I will turn to one instance of Heideggerian thinking at work. This concerns a contemporary project to achieve an unconditioned and universally valid theoretical knowledge.

THE PRE-THEORETICAL CONDITIONS OF THEORY

For some thirty years, Hubert Dreyfus has drawn on Heideggerian thinking to make fundamental criticism of projects in Artificial Intelligence (AI), understood in the sense of the attempt to represent – and hence for some to 'explain' – intelligent human behaviour by modelling it on a computer, that is as the operation of a complex but limited set of precise algorithms. The important point for us here is not computer science *per se* but the way in which assumptions in AI are a supremely clear example and a putting to the test of crucial features of the 2,500 year philosophical tradition that Heidegger attacks (what he terms 'Western metaphysics'), a tradition he saw as culminating in cybernetics and information theory.

Since Socrates and Plato philosophers and later scientists have assumed that to have a rationally grounded knowledge of something means to have a transparent and self-consistent formulation of its under-lying principles. It is held that rational inquiry should set out to define the universally applicable concepts and precise logical relations that should ground the perception and understanding of things. René Des-cartes (1596–1650), writing at the time of the emergence of modern science, argued that any problem might be analysed into basic elements and all human knowledge deduced from first principles. The proposi-tion became almost axiomatic that what is truly real is only what we can know with the intellect and with mathematical certainty. Phil-osophy comes to be understood as a foundational enterprise – the securing of foundations that permanently ground inquiry and anchor culture in the truth, becoming ideally a tribunal of reason and final arbiter of competing claims to truth or to right.

Pulling up that anchor, Heidegger turns to a reconsideration of our day-to-day ordinary, taken-for-granted understanding of things and each other. Tradition takes it as read that understanding the world and being competent in its activities depends upon having an effective inner model of the world and fluency in manipulating it from one context to another. At issue is what can be called 'theoreticism' – the crucial assumption that understanding consists in having an implicit or explicit theory of what is being understood, that all human behaviour is a kind of know ing in some sense. Thus the more efficient your inner logic, the better your competencies and the more you understand the world. Computer modelling and the building of would-be intelligent machines put these seemingly innocuous assumptions into practice. If we can state our rela-tion to things in a clear self-consistent theory, it is argued, then we can also embody that theory in a device; correlatively, trying to build such a device may be the best way to construct a workable theory.

This may seem all very reasonable, but the fact is that AI in this sense was a dismal failure. To unravel why is to approach several crucial Heideggerian arguments. Later, these will open up issues far broader than that of competing models of human rationality.

For AI, the problem is the everyday, that is, the non-reflective understanding of things that people take for granted. Computer science remains far less daunted in programming a computer to play chess at grand-master level than modelling even the basic task of recognizing and picking out the various chess pieces from the box or from a jumbled heap. Why is this? Let's take a hypothetical case, the theoretical model-ling of the understanding of a straightforward English sentence:

Because of the strike, she was unable to repair the lock in time to be able to leave for her holiday.

The issue here is that what is obvious for us is actually multiplicitous and extraordinarily subtle when it comes to thematizing it in a way that spells out every element involved in the way a computer would require. For instance, let us unpack the simple words 'unable' and 'able' ('. . . she was unable to repair the lock in time to be able to leave for her holiday'). The normal understanding of the sentence – though nowhere explicit in its terms – would include the fact that the woman cannot repair the lock herself. We know that this job usually requires a locksmith, and also that most people are not locksmiths. So we probably read the verb 'unable' in the sense of her not succeeding in finding a qualified person in time ('she was unable to repair the lock in time to be able to leave . . .'). We would probably reject the possible meaning that the strike somehow hindered her own skill in repairing locks herself. Our understanding of the sentence is confirmed, without our even thinking about it, by reference to a 'strike': we infer, again without being told explicitly, this means a strike of people qualified to effect the repair, or of people necessary to them in some way. In fact, when we pause to unravel it, even the most mundane sentence or action draws on a vast and inchoate mass of assumed understanding that gets bigger the more one tries to explicate it. Thus, when we come to the word 'able' later in the same sentence we understand at once that it refers to a different sort of capability, not a physical one but a psychological one: she is doubtless perfectly capable of leaving for her holiday with the door broken if she wanted to, but is not 'able' in the sense of feeling she cannot risk it. Understanding this inability also requires an indefinite amount of background knowledge about how human beings live, for instance about housing, about risk of theft, which in turns implies understanding of notions of property, of law, etc. This analysis could go on, unravelling further and further layers of what for us is obvious in this obvious sentence – that the woman is dealing with the house she lives in for instance. The point is that all of these things are evident to us, even to the extent that this spelling them out seems slightly absurd, yet, decisively, this also shows that the modes of understanding at issue are so subtle and multi-layered that they could probably never be modelled in the kind of self-contained formalized theory required by a digital computer.

What are the implications of this for theoreticism? Quite simply that it is wrong. Competence in getting about the world is not necessarily the application of some inner theory of it. Much human understanding depends upon an implicit, non-thematized shared mode of being – to recognize what a holiday is involves a sense of what work means, and to *need* a holiday or to feel tired. This involves not some theory of the concept 'holiday' but an empathetic sense of the embodied human world, its limits, its weariness and its recreations. This sense is not a theory at all. In fact, if one unravels it, everything in the sentence involves that sort of understanding at some level. Fear of theft relates to the need for bodily shelter, for provisions and equipment for life. These in turn relate, along with the need for a holiday, to a sense of a finite life's day to day energies and goals, its 'care' in Heidegger's sense of its concern for its own existence, and always, implicit but funda-mental, the possibility of death, that life is not infinite. '[I]n the last analysis all intelligibility and all intelligent behaviour must hark back to our sense of what we *are*, which is, necessarily, on pain of regress, some-thing we can never explicitly *know*' (Dreyfus and Dreyfus 1986: 81). Heidegger's name for what we *are* in this sense is *Dasein*. The term is colloquial German, meaning 'existence', literally 'being there', though its misfortune is to sound in English like a technical term. A 'vague aver-age understanding of being' (BT: 25) is given us in advance, for it is what makes up our *existence* in the first place.

(To anticipate, such non-reflective, non-theoretical understanding is the element of poetic language, e.g. how, for instance, would AI model Sophocles' line, in the dramatist Tom Stoppard's version: 'Love, said Sophocles, is like the ice held in the hand by children' (Stoppard 1997: 43)?)

Even as we go about such mundane activities as locking and closing doors we are not necessarily employing any sort of theory as to what we are doing any more, say, than walking or reading a line of poetry is the externalization of a theory of locomotion or a theory of poetics. Surprisingly, then, it is such utterly obvious, unthinking understanding that makes up what is essential and mysterious about human intelli-gence, not those complex operations of arithmetic or symbolic thought we value so much. (See Beth Preston (1993) for a further develop-ment of Hubert Dreyfus's Heideggerian argument.)

It is time to introduce some Heidegger more directly. What does this failure of AI show? First, that human existence involves a vast range of contextual knowledge which is inherently unformalizable, i.e. not just something very complicated but not the kind of thing that could ever be totalized into a set of algorithms in the first place. It is in Heidegger's words a 'background of . . . primary familiarity, which itself is not conscious and intended but is rather present in [an] unprominent way' (H: 189). We bring with us, even in the simplest kinds of task or statement, a sense of a 'world'. 'World' is one of the major terms in Heidegger's thinking, in the early work often close in meaning to 'being'. It means no particular entity (it is not the planet or the globe itself) but is that presupposed and disregarded space of familiarity and recognition within which all the beings around us show themselves, *are* for us. That is to say, Heidegger's concept of 'world' is close to the common meaning of the term when we talk about 'the world' of the Bible, or the 'world' of the modern Chinese or modern English – i.e. the fundamental understanding within which individual things, people, history, texts, buildings, projects cohere together within a shared horizon of significances, purposes and connotations. One might use the term 'world-view', but this falsely suggests that a 'world' is a particular stance that people or individuals hold inside their heads, as representations, rather than the more fundamental shared disclosure of things within which they find themselves in all their thoughts, practices and beliefs, providing the basis even of their self-conceptions and suppositions.

Our sense of the world is not at heart a 'theory' of it, even implicitly: it is something we 'know' in a non-reflective way simply from our everyday existence. Recounting his various confrontations with workers in AI over the years, Hubert Dreyfus recalls: 'Explaining Heidegger, I continued to assert that we are able to understand what a chair or a hammer is only because it fits into a whole set of cultural practices in which we grow up and with which we gradually become familiar' (Dreyfus and Dreyfus 1986: 5). Another way to put this would be in terms of the pre-theoretical conditions of theory. Heidegger's criticism is of the dominance and primacy of the *theoretical* in Western life. This does not refer only to the making of theories. Its target is the fundamental attitude on which theorizing is based – the notion of '*theoria*' in its original Greek sense of a neutral, detached, impartial observation, the so-called 'view from nowhere'. This seems innocent enough, even desirable, but Heidegger's interest is in the way the would-be theoreticist stance arises out of another mode of understanding which it yet denies: this is the practical, pre-reflective understanding of the world and each other in which we actually live, as engaged beings going about our daily tasks.

THE VIEW FROM NOWHERE?

We can draw on the example of AI again to instantiate another strong feature of much of Western metaphysics, one that has again come to pervade common sense. If we talk of the nature of knowing, or of thinking about or perceiving some object, we almost always pose the issues in the following way: that there is a mind or consciousness on the one side and a realm of things and other minds on the other, and that knowing or perceiving mean the taking of representations of things 'out there' into the realm of the mind. This is a very familiar dualism, one of 'mind' and 'reality', 'subject' and 'object'. Most of the major questions of epistemology (the theory of knowledge) are about negotiating this divide – how for instance, can we be assured that our representations of things, whether in thought or language, really do correspond to what is 'out there?' After all, it seems, all we ever know of reality is our own representation of it. In AI, the issue, of course, becomes how to give the computer cognitive representations that do correspond to things and which it can also manipulate in such a way as to give it a secure understanding of them.

Heidegger's aim is not to provide yet another argument about such problems in the philosophy of perception or of language. He disputes the basis upon which they seem to emerge as intractable problems in the first place. In this way, Heidegger's thinking is 'therapeutic' in the sense given by Ludwig Wittgenstein (1889–1951) when he claimed that the point was often not to address the 'problems of philosophy' on their own terms, but to undo the mental entanglements that had led some to conceive that there was a 'problem' in the first place (Wittgenstein 1974a: 133). In relation to the dualist epistemology carried over by AI – according to which knowledge is a matter of elements 'in' the mind representing things 'out' there – the point is to get away from the starting place, the false picture of a mind on one side facing a world on the other. As consideration of the pre-reflective kinds of 'knowledge' and 'understanding' tells us, this starting place is already an impossibly abstract and distorted image of what our situation actually is. Heidegger's conception of existence sidesteps such dualism at once. A pivotal argument of *Being and Time* is that to exist means to have, to be in, a world – *always already*. The human self is not some enclosed inner realm on the one hand facing an outer world on the other. *Dasein* is simply '*Being in the* world': 'self and world are the basic determination of the Dasein itself in the unity of the structure of being-in-the-world' (BP: 297).

It is not spectating consciousness which makes up our primary relation to entities. We often, indeed usually, act or speak without an especially focused consciousness of what we are doing (walking, conversing, using some tool). Our being in the world is never primarily the objective, decontextualized theoretical gaze of the philosophical tradition. Our understanding always arises out of a specific situation, and always brings with it some attunement or other. By 'attunement' (*Stimmung*), Heidegger does not mean some fleeting emotional state, but a general unthematized sense of things as a whole, the pervasive colouring under which they show up as mattering or not mattering. Such attunement is a basic constituent of our world-hood – it is impossible, if one is alive, not to be attuned in some way or another. It is why certain features of the environment stand out for us as relevant, while others are just not noticed. In the case of the broken lock, for instance, it is a mild sense of fear that attunes or highlights the woman's familiar world, determining her decision not to leave her house yet (see BT 179–82).

Heidegger's thinking has some counter-intuitive effects – hardly surprising if one accepts that his target is what seems to the modern West self-evident or obvious. One thing that may seem obvious is that understanding any phenomena, such as the workings of the brain, speaking a language or locking doors, involves breaking down the thing to be understood into smaller elements and the laws of their interaction. This hardly seems controversial: taking something apart to understand how it is put together now seems like common sense, at least to any modern westerner. The pertinent term here is *reductionism*. As a philosopher of AI writes: 'the overall intelligence is explained by analysing the system into smaller (less intelligent) components. . . . That's the paradigm of cognitive science' (Haugeland 1985: 117).

How does Heidegger contest this basic assumption? In one of his early lectures, of February 1919 at Freiburg, Heidegger brings the attention of his audience to the most commonplace experience, that of coming into the room where the lecture is now happening:

> You come to this lecture room as usual, at the usual hour, and go to your usual place. You hold on to this experience of your 'seeing your place', or else you can likewise put yourself in my place: entering the lecture room I see the lectern. . . . What do I see: brown surfaces intersecting at right angles? No, I see something different – a box, moreover a biggish box, with a smaller one built upon it. No, that's not it at all, I see the lectern at which I am to speak.

This litany of the obvious soon explains itself. Heidegger is attacking the reductionist, mind-as-data-processor model of perception. The customary theoreticist perspective is that there is a neutral perception, a set of discrete sense data (size, colour, distance, etc.) and that the mind quickly correlates and works on these to interpret, say, 'brown surfaces intersecting at right angles' as a lectern or that particular configuration of colours and shapes as my friend Henry and so on. But in fact, we do not perceive in that way:

> It is not as if I first saw brown intersecting surfaces, which subsequently present themselves to me as a box, then as a speaker's desk, and next as an academic speaker's desk, a lectern, as if, in a manner of speaking, I were sticking the lectern element on the box like a label. All that is bad, misinterpreting interpretation, a deviation from purely gazing into the experience. I see the lectern at a single stroke, as it were.

I see first 'lectern': I can then, if I wish, subsequently analyse this into sense data, relations etc. We live in a world in which the meanings of things are available to us first. Counter-intuitively (at least for the reductionism now taken as normal), a sense of the whole in some sort precedes the parts of which it might seem constructed. Heidegger's view is a *holism*, i.e. the sense of things overall precedes and makes possible a grasp of the relevance or the implication of specific parts. The individual perception is already part of an encompassing implicit understanding of the whole context:

> I don't see it in isolation, I see the lectern adjusted too high for me. I see a book lying on it, directly disturbing to me . . . I see the lectern in an orientation,

in a lighting, against a background. . . . In this experience of the lectern-seeing, something presents itself to me from an immediate environment. . . . Living in an environment, it means to me everywhere and always, it is all of this world, it is worlding.

(GA 56/7: 71–2; trans. from Safranksi 1998: 94–5)

This is essentially the point made earlier, that the 'world' is what is overlooked, even as it is presupposed, by the theoreticist stance:

World is understood beforehand when objects encounter us. It was for this reason we said that the world is in a certain sense further outside than all objects, that it is more objective than all objects but, nevertheless, does not have the mode of being of objects.

(BP: 299)

So, we do not face a lot of neutral data, some purely objective 'outside', from which we then build a world. By the same token, we cannot withdraw ourselves into some purely 'inside' realm of detached consciousness from which we might look out at our involvements from a distance. To see that human existence is necessarily 'Being-in-the-world' makes nonsense of such an opposition of inner and outer. Such holism, as we shall see, informs Heidegger's turn to art as a non-theoretical mode of knowledge. A lecture course of 1955–6 argues: 'Of course we hear a Bach fugue with our ears, but if we leave what is heard only at this, with what strikes the tympanum as sound waves, then we can never hear a Bach fugue. *We* hear, not the ear' (PR: 47).

Contrast this pre-reflective notion of world with the reductionist theoreticism of AI, that is, with its efforts to build some model of human understanding out of the combined workings of simpler models of bits of it. Such efforts lead to an insuperable impasse. Dreyfus criticizes Roger Schank's efforts to model human understanding and learning as the application of a set of precisely defined 'mini scripts', concluding:

Any learning presupposes [a] background of implicit know-how which gives significance to details. Since Schank admits that he cannot see how this background can be made explicit so as to be given to a computer, and since the background is presupposed for the kind of script learning Schank has in mind, it seems that his project of using preanalysed primitives to capture common sense understanding is doomed.

(Dreyfus 1981: 191–2)

We encounter a circularity known as the 'hermeneutic circle', i.e. a circularity in the act of interpretation. It works like this: how can you recognize and judge some specific factor in a situation or text without a general sense of the situation or text overall, yet how can you have this overall sense without somehow first ascertaining its parts? AI finds itself in a cul de sac of circularity: in order to take even its first step it needs to assume the very thing it wants to explain. Dreyfus writes: 'what counts as relevant depends on the current context. But how we classify the current context itself depends on the relevant information. This circularity does not seem to be a problem amenable to successive approximations since the problem is how to get started at all' (Dreyfus 1998: 209). How could a computer be programmed to pick out what is relevant or not in an everyday situation, such as that instantiated in the sentence about the broken lock? For a human being, however, the problem of 'how to get started' does not arise in this way: we are necessarily, as *Dasein*, always already in some situation, attuned to some things mattering and others not.

This should not be read as an attack on the natural sciences. Heidegger's early training was partly in science and mathematics. The target is *scientism*, the notion that the natural sciences offer the only genuine form of understanding, and ought to be sole ground of any other. Heidegger is attacking the 'unjustified absolutization of the theoretical' (GA 56/7: 88), its objectification of a more fundamental access to things which it actually presupposes even as it denies that it does so. Scientific objectivity remains intact, but as the methodological standard appropriate for some kinds of investigation, not as the sole measure of legitimate knowledge.

TRUTH AS CORRECTNESS AND TRUTH AS UNCONCEALMENT

A crucial issue, of course, is 'truth'. Since Aristotle, truth has been taken to name, simply, the relation of a judgement or proposition to reality. A statement is true if it corresponds to the state of affairs it describes ('The lock is broken' is true if it refers to a situation that shows a broken lock). This is all very unsurprising but in fact, as Heidegger shows, a decisive element of the question has already been overlooked. This so-called correspondence theory of truth correlates judgements on the one hand and a realm of objects on the other:

> Truth means today and has long meant the agreement or conformity of knowledge with fact. However, the fact must show itself to be fact if knowledge and the proposition that forms and expresses knowledge are to be able to conform to the fact.
>
> (PLT: 51)

In other words, how could there be any perception of the correspondence of a judgement and things unless 'truth' in another, deeper sense were not already available to us, unnoticed. The point is simple. We could not judge if the proposition 'x is y' were either true or false if neither x nor y were not made apparent to us, unconcealed in some way as such or such, and this disclosure is a necessary condition for any correlation of objects and judgements about them:

> With all our correct representations we would get nowhere, we could not even presuppose that there already is manifest something to which we can conform ourselves, unless the unconcealedness of beings had already exposed us to, placed us in that lighted realm in which every being stands for us and from which it withdraws.
>
> (PLT: 52)

In other words, truth in the sense of correctness is secondary in respect of truth as what Heidegger calls *aletheia*, the Greek word generally rendered as 'truth' but more literally 'uncoveredness', 'unconcealment'. Heidegger points out the privative alpha in the ancient Greek word, *a-letheia*, designating lack of *lethe* or concealment. This is not pedantry about ancient Greece: rather 'We are reminding ourselves of what, unexperienced and unthought, underlies our familiar and therefore outworn notion of truth in the sense of correctness' (PLT: 52). Were no thing unrevealed for us there could be no 'truth' in the accepted sense of correspondence.

This unconcealment of things is not of course something human beings make, it is where they find themselves:

it is not we who presuppose the unconcealedness of beings; rather, the unconcealedness of beings (Being) puts us into such a condition of being that in
our representation we always remain installed within and in attendance upon
unconcealedness.

(PLT: 52)

Yet in the philosophical tradition it is that secondary notion of truth
that dominates: 'Truth as disclosedness and as being-toward uncovered
entities . . . has become truth as agreement between things which are
present-at-hand-within-the-world' (BT: 267–8).

By the mere fact of existing, we already 'understand something like
Being' (BT 39). So 'being', for Heidegger, names this openedness, or
'clearing', that realm of unconcealment whereby a world of particular
beings appear to us. Being, provisionally defined, is 'that on the basis
of which entities are already understood' (BT, 25 6).

all [human] comportment is distinguished by the fact that, standing in the
open region, it in each case adheres to something opened up *as such*. What
is thus opened up, solely in this strict sense, was experienced early in Western
thinking as 'what is present' and for a long time has been named 'being'.

(P: 141)

It is within this openedness that truth in the sense of unconcealedness (of *aletheia*) holds sway. On the other hand, truth in the sense of
correspondence is a correlate of the false abstracted conception of the
world as a realm of neutral objects which the mind then 'represents'
or processes. Truth so conceived is removed from our pre-reflective
relation to the world and technicized into a logical property of certain
sort of propositions. Thus a proposition like 'The lock is broken'
abstracts from the whole context that makes a lock what it is – the
door, the building, notions of security, practices of living etc. – as well
as any sense of why it should matter whether a lock is broken or not.
It is this un-worlded, technical notion of truth that dominates the kind
of analysis of propositions that makes up the so-called 'analytic philosophy' still so powerful in the Anglophone academies.

Heidegger is not denying then 'that truth exists', nor is he arguing
that natural science has no more than the status of one cultural practice amongst others, or that all systems of thought or interpretations of life are 'merely relative' etc. or other clichés of so-called

postmodernism. But he is arguing that all theories of human life are made possible by a pre-theoretical relation to being that must always be assumed but which could never be fully conceptualized. Even as it seeks to undermine the claims of traditional philosophy or the dogmatisms of some natural scientists, Heidegger's thinking is clearly committed to the some interpretations being more valid than others. Heidegger is a 'realist' in the technical philosophical sense of assuming a reality that precedes all human formulations (for Heidegger, it is one of the egotistical absurdities of philosophical reason to imagine that the existence of an 'external world' somehow requires its proof). However, his relentless attack on the fantasy of our achieving a truth which would be ahistorical and self-grounding means that no interpretation, including his own, can or should be called final.

SUMMARY

Western thought and 'common sense' tend to assume that our pre-reflective everyday understanding of things, precisely because it cannot be fully formalized, is somehow inadequate or merely irrational, to be justified by redescription in purely theoretical terms as soon as possible. Hence we hear cries such as 'the problem with consciousness is that we don't yet have a comprehensive theory of how it works' etc. Heidegger argues against a whole tendency of Western thought to valorize theoretical understanding as the only true mode of understanding. He homes in on what actually happens in the most ordinary everyday experience, demonstrating that our basic forms of knowledge are non-conceptual. Simply by existing a human being has a mode of access to the world that could never be rendered fully explicit in a theory. Such understanding is holistic, i.e. it is given all together or not at all. It cannot be grasped by the dominant technological assumption that understanding something means breaking it down into its components – this is why, for instance, in Hubert Dreyfus's application of Heidegger's arguments to the field of Artificial Intelligence, a digital computer could never be constructed with the kind of holistic, everyday understanding of contexts and situations that human beings take for granted.

The theoretical attitude, contemplating the world, tries to posit it neutrally, as just there, something simply present at hand whose elements can be measured and their precise laws of interaction determined. Yet Heidegger demonstrates that such a notion of objectivity is already an interpretation: it abstracts only certain aspects from the world we inhabit and then posits them as more truly real than the others. Such a stance instantiates a mode of interpreting what beings really are that has been dominant in Western life since the Greeks (what Heidegger terms 'the determination of being as presence'). Heidegger's aim is to question and undo this, demonstrating its unacknowledged dependence on the kind of pre-reflective holistic understanding it purports to explain.

Heidegger does not offer a new systematic theory of the world, according to the engineering model of understanding. He works to render explicit what we already understand prereflectively, invisible merely because so deeply taken for granted, even by centuries of philosophers and scientists. As later chapters will consider, it is by working at this normally unconsidered but utterly fundamental level of the pre-reflective and the 'obvious' that art, for Heidegger, acquires its power and importance.

2

DEEP HISTORY
(*GESCHICHTE*)

Human beings are essentially historical. They are born into an environment already formed by multiple layers of interpretation and tradition, even down to the most seemingly immediate sense of things and of the 'I' that perceives and thinks them. Heidegger's summary statement that '*The essence of Dasein lies in its existence*' (BT: 67) means that our lives do not express some pre-given, timeless human nature. We *are*, essentially, that nexus of practices, assumptions, prejudices, habits and traditions that make up the everyday experiences and actions in which we find ourselves: 'One *is* what one does' (BT: 283). But that 'world' in which we find our existence is not static: basic attitudes and assumptions alter. They alter in ways that cannot be calculated or predicted. This makes up Heidegger's crucial notion, 'the history of being' (*Seinsgeschichte*). It can conveniently be expressed by the phrase 'deep history'.

The 'history of being' is the context for all Heidegger's thinking about art, literature and cultural debate.

The word 'history' (*Geschichte*) here is as specific to Heidegger as is the word 'being'. It is expounded most fully in lectures given in the later 1930s (N; also Heidegger 1975b) and the 'Letter on Humanism' of 1945. Heidegger is exploiting the fact that German has two words for history, '*Historie*' and '*Geschichte*.' *Historie* names the familiar sense of history as the study and narrating of the past, as conceived by historiography or historiology – the sequence of events and facts that have come and gone. It determines history as 'a mere chronicle . . . an unfolding sequence of unambiguous realities that are now over and done with' (Rée 1998: 48). This is also the sense of history dominant, for instance, in much contemporary literary criticism (Dickens and his age, Wordsworth and the French Revolution, or innumerable such projects that put a text back into its context as into a box). *Geschichte*, on the other hand, names something less familiar and more profound. *Geschichte* means 'history' as when we say in English that such or such an event or decision was 'historical': i.e. it altered things in such a way that we are still living inside the space it opened up, just as, say, the modern West still inhabits a world in which Christianity has been a decisive, 'historical' force, whether one believes in Jesus or not. Historical in this way are (not 'were') those fundamental ways of thinking and being in which Western humanity has dwelled and understood itself since ancient Greece. For Heidegger, archaic and classical Greece was simply the 'beginning', and we are still living out the consequences of the fundamental modes of thought established there. 'The history of being is never past but stands ever before us; it sustains and defines every *condition et situation humaine*' (P: 240). The beginning then is not some datable point in time that historiography might map out as a starting point long left behind, as if time were an unfolding road or race track. 'The beginning *exists* still. It does not lie *behind us*, as something long past, but it stands *before* us' (Self: 32).

Within this essential unity of Western destiny, however, huge shifts must still be recognized. The world in its crucial features 'is' in a different way for an ancient Greek, for a medieval monk and for a modern Westerner. What each sees and understands in the simplest object such as a river will differ, for the world – the whole sense of being human – in relation to which the river appears will differ drastically between one epoch and another.

Each epoch is dominated by fundamental assumptions about things, principles so deep that are usually not even apparent – except retrospectively from another age. Heidegger's deconstruction of these epochs means the destabilizing of their 'givenness' or self-evidence. What really matters historically then, is the unthought, seeming obviousness of things at various times. The truly decisive events in history (*Geschichte*) are not battles and the rise and fall of dynasties. They are little noticed changes, behind our backs but affecting everything, in our taken for granted sense of what things fundamentally are or, to put it differently, 'The rare and simple decisions of history spring from the way the original essence of truth essentially unfolds' (P: 146).

Such shifts are not something any individual or society can direct: they are where they already find their existence. Although, there is no human control over deep history in this sense, its changes do in retrospect form a general tendency, culminating for Heidegger in the pervasive nihilism and spiritual emptiness of the modern West. Heidegger schematizes this tendency as 'the oblivion of being'.

NIHILISM

The sustained purpose of Heidegger's work was the overcoming of nihilism. The term is from the Latin *nihil*, meaning 'nothing'. The nineteenth-century thinker Friedrich Nietzsche, in making the famous – now cliché – pronouncement that 'God is dead', was making explicit the increasingly dominant sense that the universe, and human life, are inherently pointless: there is no 'true world' for our knowledge to discover and no permanent values beneath the show of appearances. All the highest values now devalue themselves.

Heidegger gives his version of the history of nihilism in *Nietzsche vol. 4, Nihilism* (N). These lectures on Nietzsche of the late 1930s make up Heidegger's most explicit engagement with nihilism (and indirectly, with Nazism, as it had come to misappropriate Nietzsche's thinking). Nietzsche's own attempt to overcome nihilism involved, in a sense, the accepting of it, taking it not as a counsel of despair but in order to affirm the view that humanity alone must remake itself according to the measure it chooses, and thus to impose itself upon things. Such a transformed humanity is what Nietzsche called the super-man (*Übermensch*).

Heidegger's analysis of nihilism strove to be even more comprehensive than Nietzsche's. For Heidegger, it is productionist metaphysics, the basis of Western life and thought, that is nihilistic. Contemporary nihilism is only the most overt manifestation of an anthropocentric, exploitative thinking that has been entrenching itself for over two thousand years. Nietzsche's doctrine of the super-man, far from being some kind of answer to nihilism, is an instance of it. It renders explicit the destructive tendency of Western thought to conceive the world merely in terms that serve to enhance the apparent power and mastery of the thinker.

Only, Heidegger argued, a thinking that goes back through the most basic decisions that structure Western thought, right back to the Greeks, will be able to disentangle itself from ways of being and thinking that are inherently nihilistic.

Heidegger traces in the course of philosophy and European civilization's basic sense of things since Greece an intensification and hardening of 'theoreticism', the drive towards technical and objectifying modes of knowledge and, with it, the oblivion of any more primordial or more reverential kind of existence: 'the familiar and well-known has become boundless, and nothing is any longer able to withstand the business of knowing, since technical mastery over things bears itself without limit' (P: 147).

This culminates in the globalized, technological civilization that Heidegger saw as a threat to the very essence of humanity. 'The limitless domination of modern technology in every corner of this planet is only the late consequence of a very old technical interpretation of the world, the interpretation that is usually called metaphysics'(GA 52: 91).

What then is the feature of Western thought, even two and a half millennia ago, which harbours such latent violence? Michael Zimmerman, glossing Heidegger, coins the invaluable phrase, '*productionist* metaphysics' (emphasis added):

> The metaphysical schemes of Plato and Aristotle, Heidegger argued, were based on the view that the structure of all things is akin to the structure of products or artifacts. Aristotle's metaphysics, for example, is 'productionist' insofar as he conceived of all things, including animals, as 'formed matter'. The most obvious example of such 'formed matter' is the work produced by an artisan who gives form to material. Plato and Aristotle seemingly projected onto all entities the structure of artifacts.
>
> (Zimmerman 1990: 157)

Zimmerman's summary highlights Heidegger's basic point: the hidden anthropocentrism of Western thought, its unacknowledged projection of instrumentalist or technological modes of thinking upon the cosmos as whole. Plato's and Aristotle's thinking still bore the traces of older, pre-metaphysical ways of thinking. This was lost as Platonism and Aristotelianism hardened to modes of thinking about the cosmos in terms that rest, inexpliclitly, on the way people thought about familiar human artefacts, i.e. all things are held to be intelligible if analysed in terms of notions of basic designs and their copies (Platonism), or in terms of constitutive forms and the material they shape (Aristotelianism).

Plato's work, far from being the guiding spirit of Western thinking as usually considered, becomes already symptomatic of decline. After Plato emerged a decisive but detrimental distinction between the 'sensible' and the 'supersensible' or 'intelligible' (i.e. a realm addressed solely to some notion of the intellect). This set up basic habits of thought from which the West has never emerged: the distinction between the realm of 'mere' change, the inconstancy of things as given to the senses, and what is taken to be their underlying essence, the non-changing template or masterplan, so to speak, of which phenomena are merely the copy, the sensible manifestation (PR: 159). To think in this way is to abstract 'truth' from the holistic, unthought experience that encompasses it. This is the determination of being as presence, driven towards an (impossible) stance that, denying its own finitude and conditionality, would establish a secure view of the bases of reality which are taken as permanent, continually present beneath the flux of things. It is a knowledge whose ideal is that of the perspective from a supposedly timeless realm. Such a fantasy of power and invulnerability culminates in the era of technology, one in which truth becomes at best a procedural notion, i.e. a calculable check-list sort of thing.

WHAT HAPPENS IN DEEP HISTORY (*GESCHICHTE*)?

History (*Geschichte*) for Heidegger is seldom (E: 77). The Second World War, he claimed controversially, decided nothing (WT: 66). The same dominance of productionist metaphysics remained as before, its nihilism intensifying with the globalization of Western modes of rationality. In Heidegger's history of being, perhaps only three events emerge as truly 'historical' (*geschichtlich*) in the guise of a change in the fundamental sense of the world, in the 'essence of truth'.

First is the translation of the Greek world into Roman Latin. The translation of the Greek language and world into Roman Latin was – is – a decisive event in the unfolding of productionist thinking. The Greeks, Heidegger argues, had lived still a relation to being in which human thinking did not take itself as the sole arbiter to which other things had to justify themselves but retained elements of a non-appropriative, non-conceptual relation to being. These are still legible in the surviving fragments of the archaic, Pre-Socratic philosophers and in the tragedies of Sophocles. This pre-reflective experience of being was not explicitly thought in classical Greek philosophy, yet it is the unthematized experience from which that thinking drew. This is why a more originary relation to things is still legible in the Greek language, as in '*aletheia*', the word for truth, which is more literally 'uncon-cealment' as we have seen, or the word '*physis*', commonly translated as 'nature' (cf. 'physics') but more precisely the 'self-unfolding emer-gence' in which individual things come forth from obscurity. In Latin, however, where '*physis*' becomes '*natura*', this sense was lost and another manner of world held sway:

> the basic comportment of the Romans toward beings in general is governed by the rule of the *imperium*. *Imperium* says *im-parare*, to establish, to make arrangements: *prae-cipere*, to occupy something in advance, and by this occupation to hold command over it, and so have the occupied as territory.
>
> (Par: 44)

For Heidegger, the Roman empire never came to an end: it en-trenched itself, invisibly and insidiously, as common sense and the unex-amined principles of Western thinking. This sort of change is the least visible: it concerns not what we see but how we see. For the same rea-son it is also 'the most dangerous but also the most enduring, form of domination' (Par: 46). In Latin is effected a decisive change in the basic senses of truth, falsehood and knowledge, and the West has lived in and from them ever since:

> What we usually call 'knowing' is being acquainted with something and its qualities. In virtue of these cognitions we 'master' things. This mastering 'knowledge' is given over to a being at hand, to its structure and its useful-ness. Such 'knowledge' seizes the being, 'dominates' it, and thereby goes beyond it and constantly surpasses it.
>
> (Par: 3)

'When Being has changed to *actualitas* (reality), beings alone are what is real' and 'being', if it means anything, can mean only 'beingness', i.e. no longer the general world or horizon within which things emerge as such or such, but merely what each being or entity has in common. The play of concealing and unconcealing in emergence (*physis*) is forgotten in favour of the things emerged. The holistic nature of human existence is forgotten and covered over. This is the oblivion of 'being' as distinct from particular beings: 'the openedness of beings [i.e. being] gets flattened out into the apparent nothingness of what is no longer even a matter of indifference, but rather is simply forgotten' (P: 147). This interpretation of reality as *actualitas* 'attains an assumed self-evidence which has remained decisive ever since' (EP: 14). So 'all Western history since is in a manifold sense Roman, and never Greek' (EP: 13), even where there has been an explicit revival of the Greeks, as in the Renaissance or in the Hellenism of later art-theorists like J. J. Winckelman (1717–68), Friedrich Nietzsche (1844–1900) and others:

> Under the influence of the imperial, *verum* ['true'] becomes forthwith 'being-above', directive for what is right; *veritas* is then *rectitudo*, 'correctness', we would say. This originally Roman stamp given to the essence of truth . . . solidly establishes the all-pervading basic character of the essence of truth in the Occident.
>
> (Par: 48–9)

A second crucial shift in the history of being occurs as the entrenchment and transformation of that Roman stamp in medieval Christianity. With Christianity a theological slant is given to the productionist basis of Western thought. God is seen as the great author and 'manufacturing cause' (C: 172 [243–4]) and 'nature' is not *physis* or the openness of unconcealment, but God's created product:

> that which is, is the *ens creatum*, that which is created by the personal Creator-God as the highest cause. Here, to be in being means to belong within a specific rank of the order of what has been created – a rank appointed from the beginning – and as thus caused, to correspond to the cause of creation.
>
> (QCT: 130)

These notions of the 'Creator' and 'creation' still betray the deeply anthropocentric bias of productionist thinking.

Finally, there is the emergence of the modern metaphysics and science in the seventeenth century, the dominance of questions of method in all pursuit of truth, and the would-be mathematization of nature. To this mode of unconcealing, being appears as no more than the totality of objects to be mastered by the technics of human knowledge, driven by its quest for certainty.

The overall shifting of epochs is not liable to human control, nor can there be any sort of logic of the transitions from one epoch to another, nor, certainly, can they be said to progress. Heidegger argues that 'the sequence of epochs in the destiny of Being is not accidental, nor can it be calculated as necessary' (TB: 9). Phrases Heidegger uses such as 'being withdraws' or 'history of being' make it sound as if 'being' were some kind of inscrutable non-human agent, even God, but this is an accident of language. 'Being withdraws' is analogous not to a sentence like 'God hid himself' but to one like 'the apple fell' or 'the wind veered'. There is no underlying rationale or motive for history. Of course, various contingencies and events can be traced as to how, say, the Roman world supplanted the Greek – as Heidegger writes such things are 'not accidental' – but that is not to find some hidden law of history. Ultimately, like human existence itself, it is without a 'why' (has nothing we might recognize as a meaning): it happened because it happened.

THE EPOCH OF TECHNO-SCIENCE

The rest of this chapter will concern the modern epoch as Heidegger conceives it. In *Der Satz von Grund* [*The Principle of Reason*] (1957) Heidegger considers a crucial principle of thought, one implicit already in Greek thought, but coming to open expression only in the work of the late seventeenth and early eighteenth-century philosopher G. W. Leibniz (1646–1716). Leibniz formulated the so-called *principle of reason*: the principle, simply, that for everything some reason or ground can or must be rendered. For Heidegger, the principle names the imperative that directs our epoch of techno-science. This is not only to require of the things that encounter us that they yield up their grounds, but it is also, of course, to posit human thinking as that *to* which things must be brought to give reason. For all its seeming dethronement of the importance of 'man', with, for example, the removal of the earth from the centre of the universe, or the humiliation of Darwin's theory of evolution, modern science at heart exalts human rationality to a degree never before conceived. Modern historiography and modern science go hand in hand with the principle of reason:

> Knowing, as research, calls whatever is to account with regard to the way in which and the extent to which it lets itself be put at the disposal of representation. Research has disposal over anything that is when it can either calculate it in its future course in advance or verify a calculation about it as past. Nature, as being calculated in advance, and history, in being historiographically verified as past, become, as it were, 'set in place' [*gestellt*]. Nature and history become the objects of a representing that explains.
>
> (QCT: 126–7)

According to Heidegger, the question is not one of science considered as simply representing an object-world but more fundamentally of a general stance towards entities. the decision in favour of certainty in representation, calculability and hence control of nature, which correspondingly appears under the guise of the totality of exploitable objects. To respond to the call of the principle of reason is to 'render reason', to explain effects through causes, to ground, to justify, to account for on the basis of principles or laws.

EXPLANATION?

With the principle of reason come certain models of what it is to 'explain' something. We can understand and explain a plant, for example, by reference to the laws of biology and evolution, and ultimately perhaps in terms of the more basic laws of physics.

Heideggerian thinking does not dispute the validity of botanical and another sciences as specific modes of capturing the world in representation, mapping out its constituents through a fixed set-up of repeatable experiments which sift and eliminate contradictions between competing theories and facts. However, it reminds us of the distinction between this technical mapping out and the more elementary unconcealment in which any such notion of truth must move, and yet which, as always presupposed, is itself not subject to the principle of reason. 'So, what's going on here with the *principium reddendae rationis* [the principle of reason]? It holds *in the case of the rose* [as on object of botany etc.] but not for the rose; *in the case of the rose* insofar as it the object of our cognition; not for the rose as it simply stands in itself and is simply a rose' (PR 38; trans. modified). As recent debates about a so-called' 'theory of everything' show, at some point, the giving of explanations comes to an end, and confronts something without reason (e.g. 'why is there something rather than nothing'). From this perspective, after all the botanical facts and conditions have been adduced, the rose has no 'reason': it blooms because it blooms.

Heidegger quotes Goethe: '"Seek nothing behind the phenomena: they themselves are the lesson"' (TB: 65). Heidegger was astonished and dismayed to learn that many modern poets also sought to explain their poems (Pet: 108).

Compare here the thinking of a contemporary cosmologist, Paul Davies:

> Yet it has to be admitted that our concept of rational explanation probably derives from our observations of the world and our evolutionary inheritance. Is it clear that this provides adequate guidance when we are tangling with ultimate questions? Might it not be the case that the reason for existence has no explanation in the usual sense? This does not mean that the universe is absurd or meaningless, only that an understanding of its existence and properties lies outside the usual categories of rational human thought.
>
> (Davies 1993: 225)

The age of modern metaphysics is necessarily an epoch of technology:

> Modern technology pushes towards the greatest possible perfection. Perfection is based on the thoroughgoing calculability of objects. The calculability of objects presupposes the unqualified validity of the *principium rationis* [the principle of reason]. It is in this way that the authority of the principle of reason, so understood, determines the essence of the modern, technological age.
>
> (PR: 121)

Despite appearances, this is not an attack on technology *per se*. The ancient and the medieval world knew technology. As Julian Young puts it: 'Rivers, for instance, those majestic, living, semi-divinities that helped measure out the different places of human dwelling, might be bridged. Yet the ancient wooden bridge unlike the hydro-electric dam typical of modernity did not change the essential course or nature of the river' (Young 1997: 175). The issue is the mode of world which modern technology projects. In modern cities, surrounded on every side by mechanism and regimented space, Heidegger often felt physically sick, responding to the environment as a kind of violence. For Heidegger, technology in the familiar sense is an effect of that general structure of re-presenting the world which has come to govern the epoch in which we live. This determines the presencing of things to human beings as what Heidegger terms the *Ge-Stell*, enframing. He means by this that the world stands enframed as an object opposed to us, a 'standing-reserve' of material and energy to be calculated and disposed of.

This enframing effects what Heidegger calls a universal expeditement, the demand that all things be challenged towards a maximized yield of energy for the benefit of humanity:

> This setting-forth that challenges forth the energies of nature is an expediting [*Fördern*], and in two ways. It expedites in that it unlocks and exposes. Yet that expediting is always itself directed from the beginning toward furthering something else, i.e., toward driving on to the maximum yield at the minimum expense.

(QCT: 15)

Technology, on this interpretation, is not the application of science. There is not theory on the one side and its practical implementation on the other. Rather, science is one manifestation of the technological stance towards entities. The essence of technology, in a famous phrase, is itself nothing 'technological' (QCT: 4). It is the *Gestell*, the mode in which the world holds sway in the culmination of productionist metaphysics.

Heidegger repeatedly denied that he wanted to develop an ethics from his thinking, understanding ethics in the rather narrow sense as the formulation of rules of guidance for relations between human beings (P: 269; see Hodge 1995). Yet one could say that Heidegger's thinking may not have an ethics but, in a sense, *is* one. The attack on the deeply anthropocentric assumptions of Western thought and religion gives his work an ethical force. It is chastening to human pride in a way comparable to the ethics of the 'deep ecology' movement. Against the traditional metaphysical drive towards a timeless perspective, a view from nowhere, Heidegger's thinking is based on an acceptance of human finitude. The Heidegger scholar Joanna Hodge writes that

'The unrestricted conception of ethics needed is concerned not just with the relation of human beings to being human but with a relation to difference, to otherness and to being in general' (Hodge 1995: 27).

What of the future? Heidegger believed that the modern epoch might endure for centuries before another mode of being might emerge. No individual thinker or any kind of political programme could achieve the kind of shift in the history of being Heidegger hopes for – after all, how anyone could affect by diktat what strikes the vast preponderance of people merely as obvious in the least thing? However, Heidegger does find slight cause for hope in an instability in the essence of the techno-logical. While history (*Geschichte*) is not under human control and 'only a god can save us' (Only: 107), perhaps the great danger of technology also harbours a saving power. For the more apparent it becomes that techno-science and the modes of social organization that go with it are not at our control, then the more the dominant mode of being in which we find ourselves – the *Gestell* as the aggressive objectification of the world as a resource for human consumption and aggrandizement – will emerge as an object of thought in itself. Losing its seeming naturalness and inevitability, the dominance of this mode of being may perhaps become less obvious for more and more people, opening the possibility of a new turn in the history of being.

Thinking, with the help of resources to be found in art and poetic language (*Dichtung*), cannot effect this change. It may nevertheless prepare for it.

SUMMARY

Heidegger's is a diagnostic reading not just of what is wrong with tradi-tional thinking about human rationality (as we examined in the first chapter) but, deeper than this, of what it means for anything *to be*, and for us to approach it in knowledge. In short, Heidegger sees the modes of knowing and being that are taken as obvious in the West as inherently also a matter of domination and control, modes that have come to set up the world as the totalizable object for a humanity conceived as the self-certain possessor of knowledge.

How have we been brought to this situation? Heidegger works back to a bias that was unwittingly present in the thinking of the classical Greek philosophers at the beginning of Western thought, a bias which has become more and more dominant ever since. In Aristotle and Plato the most fundamental categories of their philosophy draw upon ways of thought suited to understanding the things most familiar to us, our tools and arte-facts. Applied to the cosmos as a whole, such thinking about what it means for anything to be is unwittingly beginning to pre-determine all things as if they were meant solely for our use or mastery. This 'productionist' bias was reinforced in the crucial translation of Greek modes of thought and being into Roman ones, losing in the process the vestige of a non-appropriative – or non anthropocentric – relation to things that remained at work, if unthought, in Greek practice and language. In the modern epoch, such an exploitative attitude is explicit in the drive to conceptual and tech-nological mastery.

Despite the variety of modes of life in Europe over the past two and half millennia, Heidegger traces a fundamental continuity in the kind of tech-nicist, productionist thinking inaugurated in Greece, consolidated by the Romans, perpetuated by the religion of the Middle Ages and culminating in our epoch of globalized techno-science. Even the Christian God offers no real alternative to the anthropocentric bias of such thinking, for Christian notions of nature as God's created product, of God as maker, and even notions of cause and effect, all bear the hallmarks of an unacknowledged interpretation in productionist terms.

This conception of the 'history of being' is the context for all Heideg-ger's thinking about art and the poetic. Do these keep open the faint possi-bility of modes of being that resist the dominant productionist modes of understanding?

3

'THE ORIGIN OF THE WORK OF ART'

This chapter devotes itself entirely to a reading of Heidegger's lecture, 'The Origin of the Work of Art', described as simply 'the most radical transmutation of aesthetics', or the philosophy of art, 'since the Greeks' (Haar 1993: 95). The text published in *Holzwege* (1950) (PLT: 17–87) is based on three lectures given in November and December 1936 (see Taminiaux 1993). The text explicitly rejects the terms that usually dominate discussion of this kind. It refuses to speak of art in terms of 'form' and 'content', 'individual creativity', 'meaning', 'artist's intention', 'aesthetic experience' or 'aesthetic judgement' or 'taste'. The essay is a rejection of the Western tradition of aesthetics and a retrieval of its forgotten sources. Instead of the familiar terms of aesthetic or critical debate, Heidegger's essay presents a seemingly obscure set of neologisms, 'world', 'earth', 'strife', 'Saying'. The reader must resist being too hasty to translate these into terms already familiar. Heidegger's fundamental criticism of received modes of thinking demands a new and radical start.

At issue throughout 'The Origin of the Work of Art' and not fully resolved by the end is the nature and potential of art works in the time of the dominance of technological thinking. Metaphysical reason is driven to place everything under the aegis of logic and intelligibility. For such thinking – ends-oriented, instrumentalist – art is left with the sphere of mere aesthetic feeling, the consumerism of personal taste and, at best, only a marginal relation to truth. The very meaning of the term 'art' in the modern epoch testifies to this: it is a realm of aesthetic experience considered separately from the spheres of knowledge and ethics. For Heidegger, art for art's sake is the death knell of art. So, ironically, is the very discipline of aesthetics, formed in the eighteenth century as the separate philosophical study of sensuous feeling.

Heidegger's essay is in debate with the claim of his great predecessor in philosophy, G. W. F. Hegel (1770–1831), made in the 1820s, that 'art is and remains for us, on the side of its highest destiny, a thing of the past' (Hegel 1993: 13). This was not to deny that art would continue to change and develop, producing accomplished new work, but an acknowledgment that the overall place of art in people's lives is now a minor one, dooming even a masterpiece like, say Joyce's *Ulysses*, to relative insignificance. Compared to the worlds of the classical Greek temple or the medieval cathedral, or (perhaps) Elizabethan drama, art is no longer formative of our very sense of ourselves and the reality we inhabit. Art, for Heidegger, is finite and something that can die. Dying, it can lose its power of disclosure and appear merely as an attractive object to be hung in museum, or toured on holiday; or it may be reduced to a small element of the education system or appropriated as a cultural asset, as 'heritage'.

So, the very possibility of effective art in modern society is questionable for Heidegger. Is it techno-science, not art, that is now fundamental to the West's outlook on everything? This question will extend to the very end of Heidegger's career. 'Heidegger, far from insisting that art plays a decisive role in every epoch, as many readers of "The Origin of the Work of Art" have supposed, is in fact seeking to draw our attention to its failure to do that' (Bernasconi 1985: 36). Heidegger's lecture in the mid-1930s forms an attempt to rescue the possibility of art from aesthetics, i.e. to hearken to art as the site of a resistance to the subjugation of being to theoretical knowledge. A subtext, which would have been obvious to the original hearers of the lecture, is also the possibility that art may offer the possibility of a genuine refounding of history for the German people, one that might redirect the National Socialist revolution, then three years old, in line with Heidegger's hopes for an active deconstruction of industrial society and of metaphysical thinking – some hope! He would come to acknowledge Nazism as irredeemable, another manifestation of the totalizing will-to-power he sought to question.

Heidegger is in line with other modern thinkers in reassessing art's very marginality in the modern world as a place of critical insight, a space that, if not placing it outside productionist metaphysics, at least delimits it. A series of strange ideas confronts the reader: that the power of a great art-work arises, in a sense, out of nothing; that it is superficial to see it as the product of an artist or as a reflection of its times; that art possesses a radically non-historical, acultural element; that its source is not primarily the human will and that it does not 'have a meaning' in the accepted way. Art, in short; does not make sense in any of the ways philosophy might wish it to. It follows that criticism and aesthetics, as subsets of philosophy, must be taken apart, thoroughly deconstructed, if justice is to be done to the perplexing otherness of the art-work.

THE REJECTION OF MIMESIS

Heidegger's essay rejects a view of art so deeply rooted that it is often passed over as self-evident: namely that the art work is to be understood under the category of representation, or imitation (*mimesis*), as when we say that a play or a novel 're-presents' or 'mirrors' a particular society or that it expresses or stands for the opinions or emotions of its author. The understanding of art as imitation, *mimesis*, a view established in ancient Greece, is so powerful that it is almost impossible to think of art, especially literature, without it: try discussing any familiar work without using the words 'represent', 'imitate' or 'stand for'. Yet, if one considers it, it is absurd to assume that something as complicated and mediated as *Middlemarch*, say, can be understood by analogy with a mirror, a bit of reflective glass! Instead, we must examine how for Heidegger, the work does not strictly refer to something else, is not a sign or even a symbol. Instead it presents its own unique and ultimately inexplicable mode of being, something for the reader, beholder or listener to dwell within and not merely something to de-code.

Hubert Dreyfus again offers some initial help. Heidegger, in his argument with the dominance of theoreticist thinking, 'holds open', writes Dreyfus:

the possibility that there still exists in our micro-practices an undercurrent of a pretechnological understanding of the meaning of Being ... involving

> nonobjectifiying and nonsubjectifying ways of relating to nature, material
> objects, and human beings.
>
> (Dreyfus 1985: 244)

A literary work may be a micro-practice of this sort:

> To take examples close to home, Faulkner personifies the wilderness, Pirsig
> speaks with respect of the quality even of technological things such as motor-
> cycles, and Melville opposes Ishmael as mortal and preserver to Ahab as the
> willful mobilizer of all beings to his arbitrary ends.
>
> (Dreyfus 1985: 245)

This is vague, but it is easy to agree that one can understand more about nineteenth-century London from the non-realist texts of Dickens than one can from many straightforwardly 'historical' studies, or more about Augustan Rome from Virgil's *Aeneid* than from Roman historians. One can also agree that that understanding could not be turned into series of propositional statements without immediately neutralizing the way the text projects an idiomatic mode of being.

Of course, Heidegger's argument goes further than this. His concern is to establish how works of art may offer a mode of truth and knowledge more fundamental than what is traditionally understood by those terms. As we saw in the first chapter, Heidegger's criticism of the traditional notion of truth (and correspondingly the notion of fiction which it defines) is that it is essentially derivative from something more basic. It is this more basic understanding that is engaged by art. Great art, for Heidegger, is involved with truth, not in the sense of the conformity of a proposition to a given state of affairs, but as *aletheia*, unconcealment. It influences the very way reality is unconcealed or appears for us in the first place, prior to being merely re-presented. To use a term often deployed by Heidegger in this lecture, the art work is not just something that comes into the open, next to other things, it changes the Open in which it appears.

The inadequacy of the correspondence idea of truth in relation to art appears from a simple thought experiment. Let us take a recognized literary masterpiece. Either a text like *Hamlet* can admit, if only in principle, of being restated as an exhaustive set of clear propositions about the world, or it cannot. Such a series of statements might consist of such sentences of decoding as: '*Hamlet* gives a close analysis of the nature of kingship, it shows that kingship is a kind of performance, the conditions of this performance being valid are. . . .' If such statements can continue until the text itself leaves no more to be said, then clearly that rephrasing is worth more in terms of truth, conventionally understood, than the language it clarifies, for otherwise one would not need to clarify it. However, it is not hard to agree that *Hamlet* cannot be so rephrased: the series of possible statements derived from it would be potentially endless. In that case we might reckon that the 'unclarified' version exceeds the mode of merely propositional truth, without being merely untrue or false.

DEFAMILIARIZING THE WORLD

Art then, is not a matter of description or representation. This is one reason why architecture is given such prominence in the essay. A building clearly cannot be seen as a re-presentation of anything whatsoever:

> A building, a Greek temple, portrays nothing. It simply stands there in the middle of the rock-cleft valley. The building encloses the figure of the god, and in this concealment lets it stand out in the holy precinct through the open portico. By means of the temple, the god is present in the temple. This presence of the god is in itself the extension and delimitation of the precinct as a holy precinct. The temple and its precinct, however, do not fade away into the indefinite. It is the temple work that first fits together and at the same time gathers around itself the unity of those paths and relations in which birth and death, disaster and blessing, victory and disgrace, endurance and decline acquire the shape of destiny for human being. The all-governing expanse of this open relational context is the world of this historical people.
>
> (PLT: 41–2)

In other words, the whole 'world' of the classical Greeks — how all things appeared to them — is projected by the temple, something we may sense even now, though that world has perished. The fact that architecture provides basic shelter already suggests the profound seriousness of art in general for Heidegger, as opening the space in which people dwell and understand things. Art here is not considered as a realm of cultural achievement, or the basis for a canon of great monuments or examples of 'creativity', nor as a manifestation of the human spirit, nor as an historical document of unusual interest, nor as a cultural force either supportive or subversive of dominant ideologies. Heidegger sees the essential power of art – stifled in the modern world – as the setting up of the overall 'world' within which and after which all these other views of art could alone become thinkable.

The first example given in Heidegger's lecture had been a painting by Van Gogh, a modern work. The painting is of a pair of shoes that Heidegger takes to be from the world of a peasant woman. Normally such shoes would be an unregarded if necessary piece of equipment in the life of this woman, a serviceable but trivial part of her world. In the painting however, the shoes, accurately imaged, are also transformed. Their usually unregarded status is altered. The painting makes apparent the 'world' in which the shoes find their significance:

> From the dark opening of the worn insides of the shoes the toilsome tread of the worker stares forth. In the stiffly rugged heaviness of the shoes there is the accumulated tenacity of her slow trudge through the far-spreading and ever-uniform furrows of the field swept by a raw wind. On the leather lies the dampness and richness of the soil. Under the soles slides the loneliness of the field-path as evening falls. . . . This equipment is pervaded by uncomplaining anxiety as to the certainty of bread, the wordless joy of having once more withstood want, the trembling before the impending childbed and shivering at the surrounding menace of death.
>
> (PLT: 33–4)

This rhapsodic example has been controversial (see Bernstein 1992: 140ff), but the basic argument is clear: art transforms the shoes so as to foreground the whole mode of being whence their particular nature arises.

Heidegger's argument seems aligned at first sight with modernist ideals of art as 'making it new', or to the Russian formalist thesis that literariness inheres in the defamiliarization or the making strange of ordinary language, letting things be seen anew rather than routinely, or to the dramatist and poet Bertolt Brecht's (1898–1956) theory of art's 'estrangement effect'. There is a crucial distinction, however. In Jay Bernstein's words:

> For Heidegger, the effect of great works is equally one of defamiliarization, but only for him the movement is not to a mere renewed vision of some particular

> ... but [a movement] from the ordinary and particular to that which lets the ordinary and particular have their peculiar shape and meaning.
>
> (Bernstein 1992: 88)

A world, in other words. Heideggerian defamiliarization has a holistic 'transcendental' aspect, i.e. in seeing its object anew it transforms our sense of the *whole* context of practices and perceptions in which that object inheres. Art is comparable here to the overwhelming experience described in *Introduction to Metaphysics*, the uncanny revelation anew of all beings under the overwhelming question, 'Why are there beings at all instead of nothing?' (IM: 1). The shoes, in the Van Gogh painting, are defamiliarized in a way that lets emerge the whole way of life to which they belong. Without this world-soliciting force, such defamiliarization would remain merely aesthetic.

THE SINGULARITY OF THE WORK

As a site of potential resistance to theoreticism, art necessarily eludes traditional concepts of interpretation or explanation. How is this? Three aspects to an answer can be schematized.

1   The resistance of a work to theoretical understanding lies in the fact that, crudely speaking, it has more the mode of existence of a kind of action or of practise than of a static object. So one cannot give 'the meaning' of a work like *Bleak House* any more than one can give 'the meaning' of a dance, or a particular way of life. To ask for 'the meaning' of the work is a kind of category mistake: it is like asking for the height of an idea or for the meaning of the French language. It is rather a matter of a singular mode of 'being'.
2   Heidegger's argument is at odds with any interpretation of the work that would understand it by reference to its author and his or her con-scious or unconscious intentions. Instead, he affirms the singularity of the work as exceeding the planning or intentional labour of the writer.

Let us turn again to an example, one taken from what is usually called the psychology of composition, though 'psychology' is a misleading term here, as we shall see. The French writer Maurice Blanchot (1907–)

published in 1955 his influential *The Space of Literature* (1982a), a text bearing everywhere the marks of a deep reading of Heidegger's essay. Blanchot is partly arguing with Heidegger but much of what he writes is often very useful for clarifying him. Blanchot's study of 'inspiration' offers a close account of composition from a writer's view. Homing in on the writer's act of composition, he highlights a crucial moment in the emergence of a possible work: that moment when fragments or scraps of the work-in-process begin to become fascinating to their own author, suggesting possible directions or significances which the writer had not foreseen but which may be read and perhaps followed through in the emergent work. The moment is that at which

> that which is glorified in the work *is* the work, when the work ceases in some way to have been made, to refer back to someone who made it, but gathers all the essence of the work in the fact that now there is a work – a beginning and initial decision – this moment which cancels the author.
>
> (Blanchot 1982a: 200)

This moment refutes at a stroke naively representationalist views of art as the re-presentation of something already given. The artist's task for Blanchot is to try to let the work emerge on its own singular terms. This is less a matter of his or her technical skill, though that is also required, than of the intuiting the potential disclosive force of the work. This seeing or 'knowledge' is Heidegger's understanding of the ancient Greek *techne*, the knowledge implicit in any craft or art. A later lecture insists: 'Art is *techne*, but not technology. The artist is *technitis*, but neither a technician nor a handworker' (HK: 13). Blanchot says that it is this ability to see the potential disclosive force of a work, and to follow it through, not technical skill as such, that distinguishes the true artist or writer.

Blanchot also follows Heidegger's rejection of representationalist theories of art. The artist, even while gazing at the environment with a view to the art-work, does not see a realm of things already there and waiting to be copied. If they are 'inspirational' in any way it is insofar as the demands of a possible work are already in play, determining what the artist sees in the first place:

> it is because, through a radical reversal, he already belongs to the work's requirements that, looking at a certain object, he is by no means content to

see it as it might be if it were out of use, but makes of the object the point
through which the work's requirements pass and, consequently . . . the given
world 'dissolves'.

(Blanchot 1982a: 47)

This means 'to remove it', as Heidegger had written, 'from all relations to something other than itself. . . . The work is to be released
by [the artist] into pure self-subsistence. It is precisely in great art –
and only such art is under consideration here – that the artist remains
inconsequential as compared with the work, almost like a passageway
that destroys itself in the creative process for the work to emerge'
(PLT: 40). The work takes on a certain force of speaking for itself, an
authority whose law may dictate, impersonally, the work's future
unfolding. Some writer's accounts of what has been 'inspiration' bear
out Heidegger, as does E. M. Forster's aphorism, 'How do I know
what I think till I see what I say' (quoted by Saul Bellow in Plimpton
1967: 184).

All Heideggerians (such as Blanchot or Derrida) would demur from
the view that the work be seen as a projection of the psychology of
the writer. To view the art-work as the product of some creative state
in the artist is only superficially correct. Remember the crucial but
initially counter-intuitive point about truth as *aletheia* or uncoveredness: 'Man can represent, no matter how, only what has previously
come to light of its own accord and has shown itself to him in the light
it brought with it.' (PLT: 171). Applied to the issue of the sources of
art this means that even as it presents to the reader or spectator a new
sense of things overall, a great poem or painting, as it works itself out
for the artist on the page or the canvas, is itself responding to an emergent vision – an insightful love poem follows, not creates, the nature
of love. Writers at work often speak of something 'there' waiting or
struggling to be said, to come into the open. So the emergent art work
opens to the artist a new aspect: things show themselves differently
within the world that the text, or piece of fine art, is beginning to
project, and the artist follows that disclosure.

So the power of disclosure itself is not our own – it is not a human
creation – but it may be harnessed and harmonized as it shows itself
differently in varying kinds of emergent work. Michel Haar writes
that the artist 'can compose only what of itself gathers together and
composes itself. Heidegger cites a letter written by Mozart: "I seek

notes that love one another"' (Haar 1993: 98). This in turn suggests André Breton's remark of 1924, in the midst of surrealist experiments with chance and 'automatic writing', that 'the words make love' on the page (Breton 1988: 286). It is in this sense, as the artist responds to, gathers or harnesses the force in the emergent text, music or brush strokes, that the most fundamental source of art is non-human, just as it is not we who bring about 'the unconcealedness of beings' (PLT: 52). The poet may only *nach-sprechen*, 'speak after' a sounding out latent in language itself.

Heidegger then rejects Romantic idealizations of the artist as prime source of the work. He is closer to the ancient notion of inspiration as the dictation of an other. The writer's personal psychology is of little relevance here, for the work in its singularity ceases to be intelligible by reference back to personal effort or expression, becoming instead something to whose emergent possibilities and force the writer listens and responds. Again Blanchot, although he differs from Heidegger in some respects, clarifies the seeming paradoxy of Heideggerian poetics. He writes of Herman Melville's *Moby Dick*: 'It is quite true that Ahab only encounters Moby Dick in Melville's novel. But it is equally correct to say that such an encounter is what enables Melville to write his novel' (Blanchot 1982b: 63).

Heidegger's then is a theory of creation, not by an artist as creator, but from out of 'nothing' – if nothing is understood literally as no-thing:

> Does truth, then, arise out of nothing? It does indeed if by nothing is meant the mere not of that which is, and if we here think of that which is as an object present in the ordinary way. . . . Truth [*aletheia* as a disclosive power] is never gathered from objects that are present and ordinary. Rather, the opening up of the Open, and the clearing of what is, happens only as the openness is projected, sketched out.

(PLT: 71)

3   A work also eludes traditional forms of explanation and interpretation because its nature is one of singularity. As he homes in on the specific nature of a work of art that distinguishes it from a piece of equipment, Heidegger refers several times to its 'self-sufficient presence'. Unlike tools such as a spade or a piece of furniture, an art-work is something which is not absorbed completely in its function. It insists on presencing as something in

itself. In this regard, 'the work of art is similar rather to the mere thing which has taken shape by itself and is self-contained' (PLT: 29).

The essay's stress on the singularity of the work leads to some striking conclusions: no explanation — whether in terms of the creative psychology of an author, the formal possibilities of language and genre, nor the ideologies of its social context — can provide a cause or principle from which the work could be deduced as an effect. This is because the work, for Heidegger, is singular in alone projecting the terms whereby it could be received, so necessarily breaking from any pre-given framework:

> The setting-into-work of truth thrusts up the unfamiliar and extraordinary and at the same time thrusts down the ordinary and what we believe to be such. The truth that discloses itself in the work can never be proved or derived from what went before. What went before is refuted in its exclusive reality by the work.
>
> (PLT: 75)

Writing on the topic of translation, Heidegger affirms something that applies more generally: 'the blind obstinacy of habitual opinion must be shattered and abandoned if the truth of a work is to unveil itself' (Ist 63). In its singularity, the work resists 'having a meaning' or being totally describable in any terminology already at hand.

THE 'EARTH': HEIDEGGER'S 'NON-FOUNDATIONAL THINKING'

Despite the novelty of its vocabulary, the depth of its scope and ambition, 'The Origin of the Work of Art' does still bear crucial features of the Romantic and post-Romantic tradition of aesthetics. One shared issue is the way a work of art differs essentially from the product of artisanal labour such as a chair or a machine. Both of these are products of a rule-bound or procedural process, the application of transferable skills. A work of art, though also a product of human action, is different. In the romantic tradition in aesthetics philosophers focused upon the possibly mysterious principle whereby art exceeds human foresight or conscious planning. They concerned, for instance, that relation to a mysterious 'nature' whereby, for Immanuel Kant (1724–1804), 'genius' exceeds a mere craftsman's talent, or, for F. W. J. Schelling

(1775–1854) and others, that unconscious power that differentiates and makes up the leap of 'inspiration' whereby the work exceeds both the conscious planning of the artist and the exhaustive or totalizing ambitions of any one act of understanding (see Clark 1997).

This element of thing-like opacity and the unplannable is matched by a new and crucial term in Heidegger's lecture: the 'earth'. The work, Heidegger argues, does not just a *set up* [*aufstellt*] a world but also *sets forth* [*herstellt*] the earth. It is site of struggle between these two complementary but adverse powers. World and earth are essentially different from one another and yet cannot be separated.

What does all this mean? Again, a good starting point lies simply in close attention to what the work does when one responds to it without presupposition. Let us return to Heidegger's account of the Greek temple. As the world projected in the temple is allowed to affirm itself, so it brings into relief the 'earth' as it withdraws and resists. Heidegger is referring both to the material from which the temple is made and the physical things around it:

> [T]he temple-work, in setting up a world, does not cause the material to disappear, but rather causes it to come forth for the very first time and to come into the Open [*Offenen*] of the work's world: the rock comes to bear and rest and so first becomes rock; metals come to glitter and shimmer, colours to glow, tones to sing, the word to speak. All this comes forth as the work sets itself back into the massiveness and heaviness of stone, into the firmness and pliancy of wood, into the hardness and lustre of metal, into the lighting and darkening of colour, into the clang of tone and into the naming power of the word.
>
> (PLT: 46)

The received dichotomy of form and material is being subtly undermined in this description. The art work, the temple, does not simply impose its own form on the material from which it is made. It enters into a subtle and elusive relationship with that material, so that the matter – rock, air, colours – is both affirmed and yet remains separate in its otherness. '*The work lets the earth be an earth*' (PLT: 46).

The 'earth' is not just 'matter' as opposed to 'form'. These traditional terms from 'aesthetics' do not work here. Again an instance from the graphic arts may be helpful – this time a very simple example of my own. Imagine a line traced across a background of mottled paper. Completed, it brings into being two distinct shapes on either side, one looking, say, a bit like a human profile with hints of other features in the mottling, the other perhaps like the silhouette of a jug with a rough surface. The picture as a whole now may seem merely to depict or represent these forms, as if they had already been there and had now simply been highlighted by a line traced along their edges. Clearly, in one sense the forms *were* already there – we are not talking about magic here – but in another they were not. To use Heidegger's terms, from out of the opaque but not shapeless realm of the *earth* – a substratum of latent but not-predetermined forms, real but non actualized – have emerged two elements of a *world*.

Heidegger's own example gives a more subtle instance of the defiance of before and after in the process of emergence. He quotes Albrecht Dürer: 'For in truth, art lies hidden within nature; he who can wrest it from her, has it':

> 'Wrest' means here to draw out the rift and to draw the design with the drawing-pen on the drawing board. But we at once raise the counterquestion: how can the rift-design be drawn out if it is not brought into the Open by the creative sketch as a rift, which is to say, brought out beforehand as a conflict as measure and unmeasure? True, there lies hidden in nature a rift-design, a measure and a boundary and, tied to it, a capacity for bringing forth – that is, art. But it is equally certain that this art hidden in nature becomes manifest only through the work, because it lies originally in the work.

(PLT: 70)

The art work then is not simply the creative projection that unconceals a world, nor, equally, does it simply arise out of the earth (as it does in Romantic ideas that art is the highest manifestation of some creative force already at work in nature). The work sets up (*aufstellt*) the world: the world was not already there and is now founded. The work sets forth (*herstellt*) the earth: the earth was already there but was not manifest. The world is formed out of and set against the earth but is other to it and is not simply derived from it. Art needs both earth and world: it is the setting forth of their relation, which is one of antagonism or strife.

The subtlety here (if only expressed analogously in these examples) is Heidegger's practice of *non-foundational thinking*, i.e. he does not argue in the traditional way by taking one of the two terms at issue, earth or world, as the first to be thought through, and then go on to determine the other on the basis of it, as its modification or its oppo-site. The need is to think their relation first and *to think both terms of the relation from out of the relation itself*. Heidegger's word for that rela-tion is '*Riss*' (which is barely translated by words like 'cleft' or (as above) 'rift'), one of several words he uses formed from the verb '*reissen*', meaning to pull or draw as well as to tear. The relation, the *Riss* is the tearing apart and drawing together whereby earth and world come into being through their antagonism. It can only be elusive because, though all-determinant, in itself it is no-thing, only the differ-ence from out of which 'earth' and 'world' become manifest. This thinking without making a false ground – a why – out of one term or the other is what makes Heidegger's holistic thinking non-foundational.

'EARTH' AND LANGUAGE

Images from the graphic arts are not too hard to follow, but what exactly is the 'earth' dimension of a literary work, something made not of stone, but of language, surely very different? And what is the 'world' dimension?

There was something about this in the passage about the Greek temple:

> the rock comes to bear and rest and so first becomes rock; metals come to glitter and shimmer, colours to glow, tones to sing, the word to speak. All this comes forth as the work sets itself back into the massiveness and heavi-ness of stone, into the firmness and pliancy of wood, into the hardness and lustre of metal, into the lighting and darkening of colour, into the clang of tone and into the naming power of the word.
>
> (PLT: 46)

So Heidegger clearly correlates the 'earthly' side of language with '*Sagen*' or 'the naming power of the word'. This is not surprising. Earth in relation to the work of art is the material out of which it is made, and a literary work is made from language. The strife of world and earth would thus be the strife of what the world projects, discloses, and the material of language itself, newly striking and opaque, self-secluding. The Heidegger scholar Gianni Vattimo writes: 'While the world is the system of meanings which are read as they unfold in the work, the earth is that element of the work which comes forth as ever concealing itself anew, like a sort of nucleus that is never used up by interpretations and never exhausted by meanings' (Vattimo 1988: 71).

Thus, as the strife of world and earth, the poem would affirm the earth in the sense of the obscure, resistant weight of language. This means partly what is more commonly called the material element of language, its acoustic physical, non-signifying reality, sounding out in the particular qualities of consonants and vowels. But Heidegger also talks of the 'naming power of language', its power of referring to things. Given the context of Heidegger's attack on the theoreticist distinction of the 'sensible' and the 'intelligible', 'earth' could not mean some merely acoustic body to which some spirit or 'meaning' was then mysteriously added. Elsewhere Heidegger writes:

> The supposedly purely sensuous aspect of the word-sound, conceived as mere resonance, is an abstraction. . . . Even when we hear speech in a language totally unknown to us, we never hear mere sounds as a noise present only to our senses – we hear unintelligible words. But between the unintelligible word, and the mere sound grasped in acoustic abstraction, lies an abyss of difference in essence.
>
> (WT: 130) (See also Heb: 101)

Insofar as any sound or written mark appears as language, it necessarily becomes far more than its merely physical presence, i.e. we say that the sound or sign 'means' something. Thus 't h e r e' considered as a sequences of squiggles, is no more meaningful than a pebble on a beach. Considered as part of a language, the marks conjure at once a possible relation to a world. Even a single phoneme or a fragmented piece of lettering found on an old wall is, insofar as it is taken as part of language, already tense with possibilities of relation and disclosure. This fundamental possibility of signifying attaches to any piece of language as the condition of its appearance. Blanchot writes of that anonymous 'giant murmuring' that is a language, a writer's task being in a way to shape it by imposing a limit of silence on its inchoate power (Blanchot 1982a: 27). In legal, philosophical and most everyday language, this murmuring of other possibilities is simply a nuisance, an effect to be minimized in the interests of a direct, instrumentalized clarity. A literary art work, however, uses language differently – precisely in not simply *using* it, for the naming power of language is manifest in it. In writing too '*The work lets the earth be an earth*', (PLT: 46).

> This setting forth of the earth is achieved by the work as it sets itself back into the earth. The self-seclusion of earth, however, is not a uniform, inflexible staying under cover, but unfolds itself in an inexhaustible variety of simple modes and shapes. . . . To be sure the painter . . . uses pigment, but in such a way that colour is not used up but rather only now comes to shine forth. To be sure, the poet also uses the word – not, however, like ordinary speakers and writers who have used them up, but rather in such a way that the word only now becomes and remains truly a word.

> (PLT: 47–8)

Heidegger is arguing that the literary work 'sets forth' this primordial power of language. This power no writer invents – who could invent the very nature of language? Haar cites the French poet Y. Bonnefoy, 'poetry is a certain excess of words over sense' (Haar 1993: 121). It is not a matter of the mere play of empty signs (or nonsense would be the greatest art!). It relates to what Heidegger calls the 'unthought' of the work.

Let us clarify further Heidegger's notion of the 'setting forth of the earth' as releasing the inchoate naming-power of language. I will close this chapter with an example of my own, helping relate Heidegger's thinking here to practical questions in literary interpretation.

Why do not, or cannot, literary works have indexes? In a late chapter of his *Legislations: The Politics of Deconstruction* (1994), Geoffrey Bennington considers the nature of an 'index'. What is an index, and what sort of considerations are involved in compiling one? Bennington refers to the traditional distinction between an *index nominorum* and an *index rerum*, that is an 'index of names' and an 'index of subject-matter'. Compiling an index of names is not a particular problem: one could nowadays do it with the 'Find' command on a word-processing program. An *index rerum*, however, is not a concordance, that is, something that simply lists almost every word. There are difficult principles of selection:

> Compiling an *index rerum* involves weighty philosophical decisions. It suggests as a basic principle that the compiler is able to distinguish between a purely verbal occurrence of a word, and a thematically or conceptually significant

occurrence. It also assumes that the compiler is able to recognize the presence of a concept or theme in the absence of its name.

(Bennington 1994: 277–8)

The difficulty is that of distinguishing the 'conceptual' from the
'merely verbal', i.e. discerning a concept, (which need not coincide necessarily with one specific word or term) as something with a clear orga-
nizational role in the some overall argument enacted by the text.
Bennington's focus here is the work of the post-Heideggerian, Jacques
Derrida: 'The compiler of the index for the English translation of
[Derrida's] *La Verité en peinture* soon realized that something about that
book made it virtually impossible to compile a satisfactory *index rerum*,
and wondered why' (Bennington 1994: 277–8). Likewise it is no accident that while literary texts may have a concordance, usually as a separate publication, they almost never have an index. In a literary text, or
one such as Derrida's which deploys literary effects, distinctions of the
conceptual and the merely verbal, the significant or insignificant occurrence of a sign etc., are all very problematic. Imagine trying to compile
an index to the first act of *Hamlet*! How could one talk about, say, 'the
poetry as opposed to the ideas' when what is specific is a struggle or a
certain generative undecidability between them?

An index could not be compiled there because the distinction
between what may be significant and what insignificant in the text is too
hard to draw. It is always imaginable that some new reader will respond
to some seemingly unmeaning element of the text, some hitherto hidden resource in the language, finding there an important element of
implication, tonality or register that adjusts the impact of the whole
work. For instance, in *Hamlet* the word 'visage' recurs quite often (more
than in any other of Shakespeare's dramas). Three examples:

[*Polonius*]   We are oft to blame in this,
               'Tis too much prov'd, that with devotion's visage
               And pious action we do sugar o'er the devil himself.

(III, i: 46)

[*Claudius*]   Whereto serves mercy
               But to confront the visage of offence?

(III, iii: 47)

[*Hamlet*]   Heaven's face does glow
                 O'er this solidity and compound mass
                 With tristful visage, as against the doom,
                 Is thought-sick at the act.
                        (III, iv: 50) (See also I, ii: 77–83; II, ii, 545–8)

Does the precise word 'visage' contribute irreplaceably to the world projected by *Hamlet*? In more traditional language, is it part of the general conceptual thrust of the text, 'what it is saying'? Alternatively, could it be replaced by another word, 'face', with no significant effect? If it were just a matter of the most basic sense, it probably could be substituted. Yet the specific word 'visage' also matters as part of the acoustic substance of the play, with its Latinate sound, as opposed to the Anglo-Saxon monosyllable 'face'. The fact that a substitution would disrupt the rhythm of these lines is already significant for the kind of semantic impact they may have: it is not only a matter of 'fitting the metre'. 'Visage' also dimly suggests 'visor' and 'vision'. . . . These speculations could go on for a while, but it should already be clear that 'visage' is the place of a certain undecidability and struggle between 'world' and 'earth' in Heidegger's sense. The 'work-being' of the work, its singular force, *is* this ceaseless struggle. It is not 'expressive' of a 'meaning' in any obvious way, but part of a texture that cannot be cut into 'sound' on one side and 'sense' on another, which is woven inextricably of the stress between them, a stress that brings each into its own in unstable opposition. So *Hamlet* does not admit of being split into an *index nominorum* and an *index rerum*. Another thing that the close attention to the earthly properties of 'visage' shows, its sound properties etc., is that is impossible to affirm 'earth' without simultaneously affirming 'world' in the form of subtle projections of possible meaning effects. The conceptual and the linguistic are indissoluble here, not in a comfortable, stable sense, but as an unresolveable and untranslatable tension. The word/concept 'visage' would be one of the countless sites in *Hamlet* where this struggle is at work. 'Projective saying is saying which, in preparing the sayable, simultaneously brings the unsayable as such into a world' (PLT: 74).

SUMMARY

Art, for Heidegger, is a threatened mode of knowledge that is being suffo-cated in the modern epoch. It cries out to be disengaged from the dominant conceptions of it, either as a mere imitation or re-presentation of a given reality, as a function of cultural debate and human power relations, as an object of merely historical interest, as merely 'aesthetic' (a matter only of sensuous beauty) or just an object of academic scholarship. Nor should art be understood in terms of 'expression', as the making outward of an indi-vidual's thoughts or feelings – the externalization of mere opinion or feeling. Heidegger turns instead to the way great art is engaged with issues of truth, making a fundamental claim upon us as to the nature of our exis-tence. It defamiliarizes, under a new, singular aspect, the 'world' of its situation, i.e. the totality of normally unthought, pre-reflective practices and modes of perception in which people live. In this way, as in the famous example of the Greek temple bodying forth its gods, great art is capable of setting forth and sustaining the most basic sense of things in a people's life. So art, for Heidegger, is always an inherently communal affair, putting at issue a society's modes of perception. It is not an object for merely indi-vidual contemplation.

To stress the way in which art needs to be rescued from dominant conceptions, Heidegger stresses the way its thing-like, recalcitrant nature always resists the grasp of any attempt to understand it in terms of given meanings, cultural implications and so on. The work's truth is always offset (like light and shade) by the depth and resistance of what Heidegger calls its 'earth' quality, as opposed to the way it projects a 'world'. We finally looked in detail at how such thinking might work in practice in a consid-eration of a literary text, my example being focused on why it is that a literary work cannot have an index.

4

THE DEATH OF ART?

'The Origin of the Work of Art' introduces one of Heidegger's most distinctive but least recognized topics, that of the death of art. This gloomy theme reappears in Heidegger's readings of poetry (see Chapter 6) and in various occasional lectures and remarks up till the end of his life. To redress the way this topic has so often been overlooked, this brief chapter will focus on it exclusively.

PRESERVATION

The death of art is an issue bound up with the way art is received in the modern epoch. So, what for Heidegger is the role of the reader (or beholder or listener) in relation to the work of art? After all, a great art work would hardly be great if few took adequate notice of it, precisely the problem of modern art.

For Heidegger the task of the reader etc. is to 'preserve' the singular world-soliciting thrust of the work, its singularity as described in the section of that name in the last chapter. Respect for its singularity means not forcing the work to be intelligible within the framework of what one already understands, whether that be the reader's sense of the work's social context or of its author's thought. To *preserve* the singularity of the work is a matter of holding open, as it were, that force of disclosure to which, as we have seen, the artist already responds in the emergent work, and not to make of the work an object on to which predetermined labels could be fixed: 'Where does the work belong? The work belongs, as work, uniquely within the realm that is opened up by itself' (PLT: 41). So 'The work's own peculiar reality . . . is brought to bear only where the work is preserved in the truth that happens by the work itself' (PLT: 68).

'Preservation', then, is the opposite of 'reader response' in any subjective sense. It does not 'reduce people to their private experiences, but brings them into affiliation with the truth happening in the work' (PLT: 68). Heidegger's notion of the reader as ideally 'preserving' work is that of a response that does justice to this defamiliarizing force of singularity:

> Not only the creation of the work is poetic, but equally poetic, though in its own way, is the preserving of the work; for a work is in actual effect as a work only when we remove ourselves from our commonplace routine and move into what is disclosed by the work, so as to bring our own nature itself to take a stand in the truth of what is.
>
> (PLT: 74–5)

In a structural sense, a reader belongs to the work from the very first, not of course in the sense of any specific person or group but in the work's necessary sense that it is *for* someone, directed outward: 'The poetic projection of truth . . . is also never carried out in the direction of an indeterminate void. Rather, in the work, truth is thrown toward the coming preservers, that is, toward an historical group of men' (PLT: 75). The work's force is inherently communal, a setting forth of a space in which a people might live. At the same time, the work is no work – does no work – if met with an attitude closed to it. Art's founding power is annulled in most official kinds of reception. 'As soon as the thrust into the extraordinary is parried and captured by the sphere of familiarity and connoisseurship, the art business has begun' (PLT: 68).

Potentially, the world-disclosing force of art is comparable to the act 'that founds a political state' (PLT: 62). Heidegger also compares the disclosive power of art to that of 'essential sacrifice', an obscure reference, apparently, to the Crucifixion of Christ as a world-altering event (PLT: 62). However, since the word of the poet is no power at all unless recognized and 'preserved' by those who receive it, the poet's founding is not a kind of diktat, to be mindlessly obeyed or imposed. It is an appeal and event of disclosure that cannot truly happen unless its readers are attuned to it. This might take centuries. The 'time of creators', is '*essentially* long, for the preparation of the truth that is some day to happen, does not occur overnight or to order, but requires many human lives and even generations' (GA 39: 56). Heidegger's ideal in the mid-1930s, far from the reality he lived, was that 'the historical existence of a people' be 'founded by the poet, organized and brought to knowledge by the thinker, and rooted in earth and historical space by the state-founder' (GA 39: 120). Ideally then, politicians would operate within the realm of disclosure at work in art and thought, as arguably Greek statesmen had inhabited the world of the temple. This was a remote even utopian hope, as old as the ideal of the philosophically led ruler in Plato's *Republic*. As we have seen, Heidegger is preeminently the thinker of the decline and possible death of art.

MODERN ART: IS ART FINISHED?

The Aegina sculptures in the Munich collection, Sophocles's *Antigone* in the best critical edition, are, as the works they are, torn out of their own native sphere. However high their quality and power of impression, however good their state of preservation, however certain their interpretation, placing them in a collection has withdrawn them from their own world.

Heidegger argues that the work of art has a finite life-span. He continues:

But even when we make an effort to cancel or avoid such displacement of works – when, for instance, we visit the temple in Paestum at its own site or the Bamberg cathedral on its own square – the world of the work that stands there has perished.
World-withdrawal and world-decay can never be undone.

(PLT: 40–1)

For Heidegger art dies once its world-disclosing is covered over with attitudes that take it merely as a source of aesthetic experience, or as a cultural or historical artefact or, one must add, when it becomes valued almost entirely as an object of critical study in universities or for public display in museums. After all, outside the academy literary culture in the twenty-first century tends to mean either a reductive focus on the personality of authors, and the cult of biographies, or it means the commodification of writer's lives and works in terms of the places with which they can be associated by the tourist industry, as in 'Hardy's Wessex', 'Housman's Shropshire' and so on.

Heidegger's great lecture, viewed in retrospect, appears as one of several attempts in the twentieth century to save art by dissociating it from the aesthetic. Avant-garde modernism, as with the surrealists of the 1920s and 1930s, had also put into practice a subversion of the merely 'aesthetic' notion of art, attempting, for example, to transgress accepted distinctions of art and reality, rendering art a privileged mode of social and political action.

Art's death is not instantaneous and is still in process. For Heidegger such dying is perhaps what modern art is. 'The dying occurs so slowly that it takes a few centuries' (PLT: 79). So what space is left in Heidegger's argument for modern art? The Greek Temple was an instance of pre-modern art, opening the question of whether modern art can ever have quite the same power. The Van Gogh painting, a modern work discussed in the last chapter, only reveals what the peasant woman already knows, albeit implicitly and non-thematically: it does not found that world, it merely uncovers it. Nevertheless, art, in this example, still makes available a holistic mode of being other than the space of calculative representational thinking. Later Heidegger was to discover the work of Paul Cézanne (1839–1906) as following in painting a path parallel to his own in thinking (Pet: 131ff).

One argument about modern art is that it enacts the failure of art's essential disclosive power to realize itself. Art becomes a space of negative cognition, i.e. its own remove from questions of 'truth' and authority renders it the space of a frustrated or denied possibility. It remains, in its tortured way, a mode of presencing other than technology, even if this mode of presencing appears largely in the mode of its own powerlessness. Writing on the communist artist Heinrich Vogeler (1872–1942) Heidegger sees a 'terror, hidden even from himself, in the face of the end of art that was to found a world, in the era in which metaphysics is dissolved in a universal technology' (Pet: 140). One thinks here also of the 'postmodern' thinker J.-F. Lyotard's (1924–98) definition of the 'sublime' as the prime characteristic of modern art (Lyotard 1989). By a sublime presentation is meant here one which presents and keeps open the fact that there is a something unpresentable. This schema certainly fits Heidegger's celebration of the great German Romantic poet Friedrich Hölderlin as the essential poet of our time, as Chapter 6 will consider.

Does art, in its essential power, still exist? Writing to his disciple, the art critic H. W. Petzet, in the Spring of 1950 (the same year as 'The Origin of the Work of Art' appeared in *Holzwege*), Heidegger argues:

> Something else: the question raised in [your] lecture – *what is* the exhibited work of art? – does not yet seem clear in all respects. The question that could be hidden behind all of this is whether there exists an *art work* at all. Or does art become untenable along with metaphysics?

(Pet: 152–3)

This puzzlement appears in Heidegger's admiration for Picasso. Is such work, however impressive, 'capable of making manifest for art even its essential place in the future. Perhaps this is not an issue for art – but then what is the work of such artistic genius? Where does it belong?' (Pet: 145). The music of Igor Stravinsky (1882–1971) raised the same questions for Heidegger ('Über Igor Strawinsky' (GA 13: 181)).

Another reason modern art is so problematic for Heidegger relates surely to what may be a questionable part of his argument. This relates to the way art's business of disclosure renders it essentially communal – it is not a matter of individual expression but of general 'world' in which a society lives. Heidegger assumes (rather than argues) that there is a close, even constitutive relation between art and the national life of a particular group. This goes beyond for example the kind of vague association made when literature is pragmatically divided up as 'English Literature', 'Canadian Literature' etc. Art for Heidegger takes place as a potentially disclosive event within the horizon formed by the world of a specific historical people (*Volk*). It arises from a particular historical people, offering them, whether Greeks or Germans, their fundamental stance in existence. It is *for* that people, addressed to their possible destiny, and it is preserved, if at all, *by* that people. In other words, the notion of a people is foundational to the processes of art in Heidegger's understanding, as it is to a whole German Romantic tradition stretching back to the philosopher J. G. Herder (1744–1803) in the later eighteenth century. 'The people' form the stage on which alone art is given a founding power, even if it be only a potential one. The notion of the people bears this function without being much analysed (see, however, C: 29–30; 66–9). It is clear, however, that a people (*Volk*) is defined for Heidegger by a common language and certainly not by race, as in the Nazi ideology with which these lectures are in debate.

This aspect of Heidegger's argument raises a question: is Heidegger's notion of art really only adapted to traditional, pre-modern, homogeneous and geographical bounded societies of the kind that have not really existed in Europe for centuries (if ever)? Is it so certain that art is national in its essence? Even if one grants that Greek Art or the work of the Italian Renaissance could be seen in this way, modern art certainly cannot. Leaving aside for now the questions of music, painting and architecture, whose language-independence Heidegger would anyway dispute (PLT: 74), surely much literature even is international in its constitution and outlook? The poetry of T. S. Eliot (1888–1965) or the plays of Samuel Beckett (1906–89) seem produced almost expressly to deride the possibility of being understood only in relation to one national culture. Both, in their different ways, are composed with reference to works in several European traditions, yet also in terms often so abstracted from specific social and historical reference as to defy being situated in any one cultural context. In a lecture of 1967 Heidegger acknowledges that modern art 'no longer originates from the formative borders of a world of the people and nation' (HK: 15), but only to see this disjunction as the end of art, and modern art as rootless and nihilistic. Heidegger here seems stuck in a form of Romantic nationalism.

Heidegger's uneasiness appears in his puzzled attitude to abstract art. Since Heidegger does not accept that non-abstract art is representational in the first place one might expect his attitude to abstract art to be an interesting one:

> Is there perhaps, behind the uneasiness brought about by a nonobjective art, a much deeper shock? Is that the end of art? The arrival of something for which we do not have a name?

> (Pet: 153)

It is mainly a negative response. *The Principle of Reason* (1957) relates abstract art and the domination of technology. Abstract art is 'a tool that unfolds the being of technology' (Pet: 66). The relation between techno-science (the world of particle accelerators) and abstract art is that neither relates to objects outside the act of its own operation, but involves the very construction of the objects they illuminate. Just as scientific experiments have become more and more interventionist and technologized, so abstract art makes itself out of its own activity:

> That in such an age art becomes objectless testifies to its historical appropri-
> ateness, and this above all when nonrepresentational art conceives of its own
> productions as no longer being able to be works, rather as being something
> for which a suitable word is lacking. That there are art exhibitions of modern
> styles has more to do with the mighty principle of reason, or rendering reasons,
> than we can first imagine.
>
> (PR: 34)

However, need this be the end of the matter? In a little known conference of 1958, chaired by Heidegger, on the relation of Western and Japanese art, one participant defended abstract art. One 'Bröse' suggested that abstract art might be seen as post-aesthetic or post-metaphysical in a positive sense, a kind of Western 'Zen' art that could body-forth the contours and presencing of pre-representational space (Foti 1998: 340–1). This idea matches Heidegger's admiration for the work of the Swiss painter Paul Klee (1879–1940), paintings far more tortured than Bröse's peaceable ideal. Heidegger seems to have discovered Klee's work in the mid 1950s (Pet: 135), and it affected him strongly enough to give rise to ideas and notes for a second part of 'The Origin of the Work of Art' (Heidegger 1993). Klee's powerful, dream-like images are usually considered a precursor to 'abstract expressionism'. Denounced as 'degenerate' by the Nazis, for Heidegger they open a new way between traditional art and merely or fully abstract works: the objects in a Klee painting do not disappear completely as in abstract art, but their withdrawal from immediate recognition forms a kind of continuous event in a world rendered newly prominent by this withdrawal. A Klee painting also makes visible the deep structures of modern human existence. Klee's *Patientin* ('The (Woman) Patient') he commended as reaching further into 'illness and suffering' than any clinical probing or medical textbook (Pet: 148). This is enigmatic but presumably relates to the notion that art can provide a holistic sense of what disease means as a disruption of the whole world a person inhabits, without mind/body dualism, opposed to the reductive analysis of merely physiological symptoms. According to Petzet, Heidegger's projected sequel to his famous essay would have dealt with Klee's unsuccessful struggle to understand what was happening in his paintings, the necessary confusion and inarticulacy that affect a great painter at a time when art is being fundamentally transformed by the domination of technological thinking (Pet: 146). For Heidegger, this transformation is such that modern pieces, however powerful, cannot be called 'works'.

Heidegger's 1967 Athens address on art worries again over the question of modern art:

> The modes by which we determine reality in a scientific world, and by the name 'science', we understand natural science, mathematical physics, emphasize something that is only too well known.
>
> By this means one is easily prompted to explain that the region from which the requirements to which modern art responds is none other than the scientific world.
>
> We hesitate to give our assent. We remain in indecision.
>
> (HK: 15)

The lecture's indecision is the very indecision in which, for Heidegger, global civilization is suspended. Is modern art no more than the writhing of a forgotten mode of being, suffocated in the world of techno-science? Amidst the continuing absorption of artistic life by the combined industries of the academy and 'heritage', this question looms, huge but largely ignored, over all the academic conferences and cultural tours.

Nevertheless, an indistinct hope remains: that modern humanity will come to feel the danger in which it stands in taking the norms of industrial society as the only criterion for all thought. Realization that industrial society exists on the basis of being locked in its own manipulations might be the first movement of a new dispensation of being, a rethinking of the unthought bases of Western thought and history at the moment of their globalization. Here art might offer a pathway: 'Does the beckoning into the mystery of the still unthought '*A-letheia*' point at the same time into the realms of the origin of art? Does the claim to produce works come from this realm?' (HK: 21).

But Heidegger does not believe anyone is yet in a position to answer:

whether art will be granted this highest possibility of its essence in the midst of the extreme danger, no one can tell.

(QCT: 35)

SUMMARY

The world-disclosing potential of art is stifled in the modern epoch, with its appropriation of art as a form of merely subjective experience, as an object for museums or for school and university study. This stifling is such that Heidegger doubts whether anything like a 'work' in the sense outlined in the 'The Origin of the Work of Art' is possible in our age. What is the status then of modern art and literature? The issue, for Heidegger, is genuinely undecided. This is not because he cannot make up his mind, but because the force of art is nothing if it is not acknowledged and 'preserved' by those who see and read, so art's future depends on the uncertain way in which dominant modes of thought and being may change. Should the over-rationalized world of modern techno-science merely consolidate itself in the coming centuries, as Heidegger expected, then the alternative, more holistic modes of understanding engaged in art will be killed off. Art will essentially have died.

5

LANGUAGE, TRADITION AND THE CRAFT OF THINKING

Nothing is more unfitting for an intellectual resolved on practicing what was earlier called philosophy than to wish, in discussion, and one might say in argumentation, to be right. The very wish to be right, down to its subtlest form of logical reflection, is an expression of that spirit of self-preservation which philosophy is precisely concerned to break down.

(Theodor Adorno)

This chapter concerns language, both Heidegger's unconventional view of language and, at the end of the chapter, the extraordinary experiments with the rhetorical forms of philosophical writings to which his thinking leads him. In between, we will have a close look at the way Heidegger reads the texts of Western tradition, his revisionist concern with what gets said or – more precisely – what gets covered over in the language of these texts.

A minute attention to language follows necessarily from Heidegger's one, pervasive intention: to free us from the numbing familiarity of productionist metaphysics. It is a hugely ambitious aim: such thinking is basic to the way the modern West sees everything. It is less *what* it thinks and feels than that *by which* it thinks and feels. Heidegger needs to undo this self-evidence:

> When tradition thus becomes master, it does so in such a way that what it
> 'transmits' . . . rather becomes concealed. Tradition takes what has come down
> to us and delivers it over to self-evidence; it blocks our access to those primor-
> dial 'sources' from which the categories and concepts handed down to us have
> been quite genuinely drawn.
>
> (BT: 43)

Heidegger aims to clarify the 'pre-ontological understanding of being' which tradition covers over, even as it must finally rest upon it. (Ontology is the name of that field of philosophy which concerns itself with the concept of 'being'). Such inquiry the Heidegger of *Being and Time* called a 'fundamental ontology' but he later abandoned this phrase as still too traditional in its implications. He also called it a 'destruction' or 'de-constructing' (BP: 22–3) of metaphysically based assumptions and perceptions, not in the sense of a violent demolition but as a de-layering of structures of the obvious. Heidegger means the 'disobstruction' of our immediate existence, encrusted as it is with millennia of theoreticist and objectivizing assumptions. This is, in effect, what we have already followed in our exercise about AI in Chapter 1:

> We understand this task as one in which by taking *the question of Being as our*
> *clue,* we are to *destroy* the traditional content of ancient ontology until we arrive
> at those primordial experiences in which we achieved our first ways of deter-
> mining the nature of Being – the ways which have guided us ever since.
>
> (BT: 44)

LANGUAGE

The crucial issue for Heidegger after *Being and Time* becomes language, and the language of tradition, what it covers over, the resources it draws from, what it reveals in its unsaid.

Heidegger's thinking on language is as distinctive as any other aspect of his work. There is nothing unusual in his seeing language as a defining characteristic of humanity. This is already the case for Aristotle in ancient Athens. If Heidegger seems strange it is because he rejects the traditional or obvious view of language: that it is an instrument whereby we represent things or thoughts to ourselves and to each other, a medium of communication. Heidegger argues that, ultimately, lan-guage cannot be seen as our tool and that – in a notorious phrase –

'it is language that speaks' (*die Sprache spricht*) and not the human being: 'For strictly it is language that speaks. Man first speaks, when and only when he responds to language by listening to its appeal' (PLT: 216). This claim, preposterous at first sight, should become clear in the light of Heidegger's general holism.

Heidegger thinks through Hölderlin's lines 'Since we have been a conversation / And able to hear from one another'. What, he asks, is the nature of conversation and what can it tell us about language generally? A first point, strange and then evident, is that language is not identical with what is said (or written). First, speaking in conversation is as much a matter of listening as it is of talking. In conversation, you must be able to hear, to pick up in the speech of the other the silences as well as the statements. ('Being able to talk and being able to hear are co-original' (E: 57)). In addition, it is far more than just a matter of a shared ability to form words and sentences. Language is not just a system of signs whose code supposedly resides 'in' the minds of its users. It is better expressed as an all-pervasive but utterly decisive environment, one which opens and maintains the shared horizon within which understanding is possible, the common world that enables people to approach and make sense of things and each other. The work of language projects a context for us in which gesture, timing, silence and so on are each part, yet none could be fully captured in a notation, a formalized system of grammar, or some taxonomy of types of speech act. 'Only where there is language, is there world' (E: 56). Even disagreements take place within an essential coming-together in language, a space without which no misunderstanding even would be possible. Thus 'We are always speaking, even when we do not utter a single word aloud, but merely listen or read, and even when we are not particularly listening or speaking, but attending to some work or taking a rest' (PLT: 189).

As the fundamental environment in which we perceive, think, talk and have our being it is only superficially the case that language is a set of signs attached to 'ideas', or that these are themselves 'representations' or images of things out there. As anyone who has studied a foreign language knows, any language brings with it its own specific world:

> In the current view, language is held to be a kind of communication. It serves for verbal exchange and agreement, and in general for communicating. But

language is not only and not primarily an audible and written expression
of what is to be communicated. It not only puts forth in words and statements what is overtly or covertly intended to be communicated; language
alone brings what is, something that is, into the Open for the first time. Where
there is no language, as in the being of stone, plant, and animal, there is also
no openness of what is.

(PLT: 73)

Heidegger's concern then is not the surface phenomena of language,
the communication within the already opened space, but with the way
language makes possible that space itself, its attitudes, attunements –
the sort of world disclosed there. Animals may or may not have their
own kind of open region or clearing (Heidegger's denial of full world-
hood for animals has been controversial (see Derrida 1989: 47ff; Krell
1992: 112ff)), but for human beings worldhood is given in language.
For instance, as we saw in Chapter 2, for Heidegger the translation of
Greek thinking and its world into Latin, into Romanness, was perhaps
the most crucial event in the history of the West. So, as that which
opens to us the world we inhabit, it is language that speaks, not human
beings. (If this still seems counterintuitive, try inventing a few words
of your own overnight and see how you fare using them the next day.)

Such a notion of language informs the extraordinary importance
Heidegger gives certain poets (Homer, Hölderlin). In his legacy in
deconstructive thinking (see Chapter 8), it informs arguments to the
effect that the language of a text may say something other than anything
identifiable with an author's intention, conscious or otherwise: 'it is
not we who play with words, but the nature of language plays with us
. . . long since and always' (WT: 118).

Given this conception of language, it is not surprising that Heidegger's destruction of productionist metaphysics should focus upon the
language of tradition, nor that Heidegger's thinking should turn to
more and more rhetorically strange and inventive modes of language
in order to try to free itself of that tradition. He would awaken in the
tired terminology of philosophical and critical thought the realization that language is at its basis an art-work, a *poesis*. It is a mode of
disclosure, not a mode of re-presentation.

TRADITION AND THE TRACE

Heidegger's statements on nihilism and the crisis facing Western civilization accord with those of many German intellectuals in the period after the disaster of the Great War. They imply the need for a complete break with the past, a notion Heidegger held till his death. We live in an 'exhausted pseudo-culture' (Wolin 1993: 18). The issue, he wrote in 1920, is 'whether from this destruction a new "culture" will emerge or an acceleration of decline' (ibid). It is the profundity of Heidegger's thinking to uncover 'productionist' metaphysics at work in every aspect of modern life and thought, even what we take to be obvious. So pervasive is it that one soon sees why the notion of a complete rupture from tradition so appealed to him. An extreme diagnosis requires extreme solutions, yet this inevitably raises the issue of Heidegger's sudden turn to Nazism in 1933, which took even his close disciples by surprise (see Chapter 7). Lest we be too hasty about the political tendency of Heidegger's anti-modern thinking, Richard Wolin reminds us that 'a surprisingly similar critique of modernity was shared by the radical left' (Wolin 1993: 18). The later Heidegger, who will mainly concern us here, sustains a radical critique of modernity, but now teaches that there is no single, simple border to cross from productionist meta physics into some barely conceivable other realm. We must learn instead – it is the only option – a patient and thoughtful transformation of the space and traditions in which we already find ourselves.

Heidegger's intervention then usually takes the form of a revisionist close reading of the philosophical texts in the Western tradition. This is to give a crucial place to the texts of that tradition and, to some extent the poetic tradition. These, for Heidegger, render legible the bases of Western history. This is not, however, to indulge in some professor's fantasy that philosophy as a discipline grounds human life, that philosophers are the unacknowledged legislators of the world. His far more plausible claim is that philosophers – and poets – bring to language the pervasive but otherwise unthematized understanding of their epoch. Such an act is necessarily always incomplete, which is one reason why Heidegger's concern, whenever he reads a philosopher, is with what he terms the 'unthought' of the thinking, that unthought matrix out of which what is explicit emerged. Heidegger writes: 'What is unthought in a thinker's thought is not a lack inherent in his thought. What is *un*-thought is there in each case only as the *un-thought*. The more original the thinking, the richer will be what is unthought in it' (WT: 76).

Jacques Derrida writes that for philosophy a univocity of language – i.e. the ideal of an unequivocal language with one clear sense – is 'the essence, or better, the *telos* [end or ideal] of language. No philosophy, as such, has ever renounced this Aristotelian ideal. This ideal is philosophy' (Derrida 1982: 247). It is a Heideggerian point. One reason Heidegger is so alien to most thinkers in the Anglophone tradition of philosophy is that he questions what is usually the first, almost instinctive gesture of philosophical argumentation, that of making one's terms into univocal and precise concepts. Heidegger does not try to reduce the terms of thinking to a clarity that would aim to be context-independent, ahistorical, as though it were a merely a matter of Aristotle and Bertrand Russell going over identical issues in different languages – the supposedly perennial 'problems of philosophy'. For Heidegger of course, the language of neither philosopher could be abstracted or 'unworlded' in that way. This is not to say that Heidegger is reducing philosophical texts to merely historical documents, as in the historicism of many literary critics, but he is reading with a view to deep history in the sense of *Geschichte*, i.e. the seemingly obvious, unthought sense of things that pervades and structures the texts.

Destruction/deconstruction will give a close reading of the texts of tradition, teasing out their dependence on unthematized elements they cannot explicitly avow. For Heidegger, 'the multiplicity of possible interpretations does not discredit the strictness of the thought content' and is not 'the residue of a still unachieved formal–logical univocity which we properly strived for but did not attain' (WT: 71). Heidegger's scholarship is usually thorough, but its goal is to open out, in the terms and concepts of previous thought, the *unthought* legible there. Listening to language, Heidegger's thinking strives to solicit from these texts a sense of the kind of world at sway there – the way 'being is said' as Heidegger puts it. So it is not a case of what Parmenides or Anaximander, for example, 'meant', but of the trace of what is unthought but marked in their Greek. We have already seen an example of this sort of attention in the way that a notion of truth as 'unconcealment' still offers itself to be read in Greek texts as *'aletheia'* (*a-letheia*), even though these thinkers are starting to use the term in the sense of truth as only a property of human judgements, as the correctness of judgements. As Robert Bernasconi explains, 'When we hear the *lethe* [concealment] in *aletheia* we are listening not to Parmenides, but to the speaking of language itself' (Bernasconi 1985: 25). This trace, not explicitly thought by the Greeks themselves, is already the sign of a forgetting of thought's unreflective conditions.

Heidegger's thinking, in its attempt to attune itself to its subject matter, the being of particular beings, is, Heidegger writes, 'in the service of *language*' (Heidegger 1989: 93; Heidegger's italics). This is, of course, a reversal of the common notion that language is – or ought to be – the servant of a pre-existent thought. 'The ultimate business of philosophy', we read in *Being and Time*, 'is to preserve *the force of the most elemental words* in which Dasein expresses itself, and to keep the common understanding from leveling them off to that unintelligibility which functions in turn as a source of pseudo-problems' (BT: 262). After *Being and Time* this sentence might need a slight modification, making it clearer that the space opened in language is where *Dasein* finds itself, not something it creates. Philosophy needs to preserve 'the most elemental words in which [being]' is said. Heidegger's reading focuses on 'basic words' (*Grundworte*) – words such as 'art', 'truth', 'being', 'nature', 'politics', 'history'. These bear 'within' them crucial and differing historical understandings of being and *Dasein*. These are words in which decisive deep historical (*geschichtlich*) shifts show up, where little noticed but colossal alterations in the human world are at work in language. The Greek word *techne* is a good example: it once named the knowledge implicit in the making of something, both in art and technology. Later these become distinct, even antagonistic.

Heidegger's attention to the texts of tradition offers a very strange and elusive kind of interpretation. It is not the fixing of what the thinkers in the tradition 'meant', nor the teasing out of logical tensions in their arguments with a view to either refuting or defending them; nor is it a so-called 'hermeneutics of suspicion' in the sense of a sniffing out in the texts hidden or unconscious motives or unacknowledged prejudices at work there. We are concerned here with the trace of what (a) was not explicitly thought, but was precisely 'unthought'; and (b) which could never have been present as an *object* of thought, for what is 'unthought' was never an entity *in* the world, but is precisely the holistic all-pervading world and context out of which particular things emerged. Such a context, and the deep history it conveys, finds its primary site in the language in which these past thinkers lived. Speaking over and beyond their conscious intention or argument, it conveys the fundamental sense of things through which they saw, and which made those intentions or arguments possible.

Tradition for Heidegger is an object of destruction or deconstruction, but this is not a simplistic gesture of rejection. After all, what else do we have to think with? The language of tradition also contains the unthought traces of its own unbuilding: 'It is simply a matter of listening to this tradition in return, and thereby examining the prejudices and pre-judgements in which every thinking, in its own way, must dwell' (P: 332). Heideggerian critique is a listening to the text and the tracing out of its limits, not a philosophical 'attack' on or 'defence' of its 'positions', as the usual military language has it. He tries to trace those limits, not as a Marxist or Freudian reading would, by setting up some meta-philosophical system which could judge and itemize its object from the outside, but by following elements of dependence in the traditional text which trouble its own theses. These 'unthought' traces in the text indicate, in David Kolb's words, 'that there is *within* philosophy a thinking that conditions its activity but does not operate according to its rules' (Kolb 1995: 66). Readers may also recognize here major features of the kind of reading associated with deconstruction under Derrida's name.

A glance at Heidegger's own vocabulary in *Being and Time* is helpful here. Whenever it is a matter of a philosophical or common sense legacy to be deconstructed the terms at issue are usually traditional ones, and they are most often Latin (i.e. Roman or medieval) in origin – terms such as 'object', 'subject', 'concept', 'perception', 'reality', and 'intellectual'. When, however, Heidegger struggles to re-express the question of being more primordially he has recourse to colloquial German, its phrasal verbs and flexible compounds, and sometimes what looks (wrongly) like mere word-play: '*Dasein*', '*Sorge*', '*Mitsein*', '*schon-sein-in*', '*vorhanden sein*' etc. . . . The vernacular emerges as sometimes closer to the unthought but pervasive pre-reflective realm than does philosophy or science, and thus as a major resource for a thinking trying to free itself from Western metaphysics. It is the unformalized language of the tradition, not its technical terms, that preserves, withholds and so keeps safe the 'unthought' from which more thematic kinds of thinking stand forth. Not surprisingly then, Heidegger sees local dialect as the 'the mysterious wellspring of every true language' (Heb: 90). In a memorial address on the writer and fellow Swabian Johann Peter Hebel (1760–1826), Heidegger ascribes the secret of Hebel's poetry to his having incorporated into literary language the characters of the Allemanic dialect. Appealing to a clue for thinking afforded by dialect, Heidegger adds (in a seminar of 1966–7) that 'Language is much more thoughtful and open than we are' (Her: 127).

TRANSLATINGS

Let us turn now to see how this all works out in the minutiae of Heideggerian reading, especially in Heidegger's deployment of translation and what looks like etymology – the study of the supposed 'root' meaning of words – in the close work of defamiliarizing a text. In his lecture course of 1942 on Hölderlin's hymn 'The Ister' (composed *c.* 1803–4) Heidegger remarked: 'Tell me what you think of translation, and I will tell you who are' (Ist: 63). One of the most seemingly vulnerable aspects of Heidegger's work is his offering of unconventional translations, usually from Greek, which he declines to defend by the normal criteria of scholarship. Yet what, after all, is the standard of correctness in the use of language, in translating from one tongue to another for instance? This question is considered in detail throughout Heidegger's life. *Introduction to Metaphysics* (1953) contains a difficult but important section on the major terms of grammar as established by the Greeks (IM: 55ff). The course 'The Ister' considers the status of dictionaries in making translations:

> A 'wordbook' can give us pointers as to how to understand a word, but it is never an absolute authority to which one is bound in advance. Appealing to a dictionary always remains only an appeal to one interpretation of a language, an interpretation that, in terms of its procedure and its limits, usually cannot be clearly grasped at all. Certainly, as soon as we regard language merely as a vehicle, then a dictionary that is tailored to the technique of communication and exchange is 'in order' and is binding 'without further ado'. Viewed with regard to the historical spirit of a language as a whole, on the other hand, every dictionary lacks any immediate or binding standards of measure.
>
> (Ist: 62)

Thus, only a thoughtful dwelling in the language world of Greek – 'the historical spirit of a language as a whole' – will enable a translator to undertake the job of finding the German that responds to the Greek. The choice of German will likewise have genuine force if it proceeds not from a bookish dictionary-led competence but from its speaker's own 'translation' into the language-world of German. This is one basis for Heidegger's repeated claim that, in matters of language, a listening to the speaking of language itself precedes the thoughtful or poetic speech of any individual. Translation becomes a place where one's own language is made to feel its finitude, even its failure, so providing a threshold to its unthought (cf. WL: 27). In other words translation is a genuine discipline of thought. It is no accident that just about every page of Heidegger's contains some work of translation in the form of some crucial Latin or Greek term with its tentative German rendering.

Translating can even bring to light connections in the translated language not explicit there, and is necessarily a kind of interpretation. Likewise, all interpreting of texts in one's language is also translation. It is in the essence of the singular power of texts by such thinkers as Kant and Hegel that they are also 'in need of translation' (Ist: 62), that is, that they resist the measure of common understanding and are set forth in language that must be worked through in its own, inhabitual terms. In fact 'the more difficult task is always the translation of one's own language into its ownmost word' (Par: 13; see Emad 1992). Heidegger himself writes in a mode demanding translation in the same sense, i.e. as requiring thought and resisting easy appropriation. Consider the following passage:

> Such need [for translation for great works of thought in the same language] is not a lack ... but rather the inner privilege of such works. In other words: It pertains to the essence of the language of a decisively historical people [*eines geschichtlichen Volkes*] to extend like a mountain range into the lowlands and flatlands and at the same time to have its occasional peaks towering above into an otherwise inaccessible altitude. In between are the 'lower altitudes' and 'levels'. As translating, interpreting indeed makes something understandable – yet certainly not in the sense that common understanding conceives it. Staying with our image: The peak or a poetic or thoughtful work of language must not be worn down through translation, nor the entire mountain range leveled out into the flatlands of superficiality. The converse is the case: Translation must set us upon the path of ascent toward the peak.
>
> (Ist: 62; trans. modified)

Internal translation, saying the seemingly 'same' thing again in the 'same' language can be just as crucial. Reformulation (*Umschreibung*), is basic to any act of understanding, in profound thought as in the most mundane conversation. All thinkers, from Heidegger's viewpoint, necessarily think the 'same', i.e. the question of being, explicitly or otherwise. Heideggerian thinking, however, with its revisionist strategies of reading and defamiliarization, aims to be a saying of the same thing (being) in its previously unthought sense. Joanna Hodge is very helpful on this point:

> The suggestion is that the text [of tradition] cannot be expected to articulate completely what it is attempting to articulate; thus the meaning to be recovered is one which is not fully expressed in the text but is indicated and gestured to as meaning to be brought into expression at some future time. The meaning in the text has the structure of an incomplete event. . . . [Interpretation] is a retrieval of a past, but a retrieval in relation to an incomplete past . . . not a completed, closed off past.
>
> (Hodge 1995: 114)

READING A PHILOSOPHICAL TERM

Let us turn now to the specific kinds of approach Heidegger employs when it comes to reading a specific text from the philosophic tradition. The use of etymology, translation, internal translation and reformulation are all found in Heidegger's lectures. I will turn here to a lecture given in 1951, on the historically decisive Greek term, *logos* (Log.). This term is translated in some contexts as 'language', but in others as 'reason' (hence forming the suffix 'logy' in 'entomology', 'biology', or, of course, 'etymology'). The Septuagint, the Greek translation of the Hebrew Torah or Old Testament, uses *logos* in the sense of the word of God ('In the beginning was the word (*logos*)'). Again, the force of *logos* is distinct from the mere 'language'. Heidegger's essay 'Logos' is devoted to a reading of the term in a Pre-Socratic philosopher, Heraclitus, who stood at the very inauguration of Western thought (*c.* 500 BC), early enough to be irreducible to productionist metaphysics.

What are all the 'translations', 'etymologies' and so on doing in Heidegger's lecture? Heidegger's overall strategy is to read the text from tradition as a 'word of being'. That is to say, Heidegger aims not to fix the sense of *logos* in the received way of making a determinate, univocal concept out of it, nor to track with his etymologies some supposed original sense from which all the others would supposedly derive. Instead, Heidegger pays close attention to the word across the multiplicitous senses in its history, idioms and associations, with a view to releasing as non-reductively as possible the kind of world or 'worlding' at work in the language, i.e. the unformalizable context of practices, beliefs, attitudes and fundamental attunements implicit there. This is to reawaken the context assumed in and projected by that language, not in the sense of the particular historical circumstances of a word such as *logos*, but in terms of its inflection of the basic take upon being at work in the Greek, i.e. Heidegger always reads with a view not to *Historie* but to deep history (*Geschichte*).

Logos then is not just the same as the Latin '*ratio*' or the modern 'language' by which it has been so often translated. To translate thus is merely to erect a mirror in which we will see only ourselves and our familiar terms of thought. Heidegger is guided by the fact that the Greek word *logos* is related to the verb *legein*. *Legein* is striking in that it may mean both to 'say' and 'to gather', as in a harvest. In fact the sense of gathering is 'just as early' and even more originary. Heidegger also refers to the striking fact that the German '*legen*' (to lay down, gather, lay before) also relates to language, the related '*lesen*' (to read; from Latin '*legere*' to gather, collect or bind together). This correspondence of Greek and German lies less in the historical relation of languages than in the imprint of the matter at issue upon both – it is appropriate to add that the English word 'to glean' is used in the sense of read (as in 'gleaning' the content of a book) as well as gathering or harvesting. Meditating upon the words *logos* and *legein* with a view to rendering explicit the 'world' at work there, Heidegger's lecture necessarily broadens its reference enormously. Gathering is not something that makes sense as an action in itself – people do not collect fruit or wheat together simply to make a heap. The making, storing, using and celebrating of bread and wine is central to the culture's whole existence. Heidegger translates himself and his readers into the historical spirit of Greek, that nexus of significances, associations, implicit practices and rituals at work there.

> The gleaning at harvest time gathers fruit from the soil. The gathering of the vintage involves picking grapes from the vine. Picking and gleaning are

followed by the bringing together of the fruit. ... But gathering is more than mere amassing. To gathering belongs a collecting which brings under shelter. Accommodation governs the sheltering; accommodation is in turn governed by safekeeping.

(Log: 61)

Such a world, as we saw in Chapter 1, must be conceived holistically.

Further research into the ancient Greek helps Heidegger conclude that the more originary meaning of '*legein*' as 'gathering' cannot simply be said to have been replaced by the more customary one of saying and talking. That *legein* (saying) is also *legein* (gathering) cannot be described a mere transformation in word meanings. For instance, to claim that *legein* as 'saying' is a metaphor or a dead metaphor would be grossly inadequate, partly because the very concept of 'metaphor' already smuggles in various decisions about the nature of the language which ought still to be at stake in our inquiry, such as the distinction between the 'proper' meaning and the 'figurative' one: 'What we have been thinking about in no way tells us that "*legein*" advanced from one meaning, "to lay", to the other, "to say"' (Log: 63). Instead, we must simply take Heraclitus, in the language he inherits, as finding 'saying' to be a 'laying side by side' or 'gathering'. In the world of Greek, these things go together. Anachronistic terms such as metaphor should be kept out of it. Thus, 'The saying and talking of mortals comes to pass from early on as *legein*, laying' (Log: 63). Language is a *legein* in the sense of 'letting things lie together before us' (Log: 63).

So what sort of a reading of the term is this? As with the terms *aletheia* and *physis*, Heidegger is trying to draw out of the Greek words *legein* and *logos* a legible trace of the pre-representational, holistic realm of un-concealment presupposed in all understanding. *Legein/logos* names the pre-rational sense of order in the world of the Greeks, the way things appeared as 'going together', that pre-analytic synthesis whereby the world gave itself as non-chaotic, harmonious in certain ways. Such 'gathering' is not the methodized sequencing of deduction or of analysis, but a more originary and holistic sense of the order of things, prior to the forming of concepts, representations, or discrete word-meanings.

For the Greeks then, being was experienced, if not explicitly thought, as the original holistic 'gathering' process that set all individual beings together in relation to each other. Furthermore, in this case, it is the Greek word often translated as language that gives us this truth, a truth precisely about the hidden power of language in the giving of a 'world'.

With its 'etymologies' and the teasing out of sedimentations of context Heidegger's thinking has inevitably been accused of abandoning the rigour of conceptual thinking for something merely 'poetic'. Such an impression, however, does no justice to what is usually a high level of scholarship and historical precision in Heidegger's work. His point is not, for example, that the etymological sense of a word is the 'true' one to be retrieved and celebrated, but to use etymologies in a process of 'internal translation' and defamiliarization, as 'hints' 'gestures' or as a 'freeing word' (WL: 241), opening up the language of the text from its dominant, metaphysical interpretation, and by so doing becoming sensitive to the mode of worlding that holds sway there, unthought. Heidegger argues: 'the experience of *Aletheia* as unconcealment and disclosure in no way bases itself upon the etymology of a selected word, but rather on the matter to be thought here' (P: 332).

In sum, for Heidegger to read the key words of the tradition, such as 'truth' or *logos* as each already a 'word of being', is to read them as a trace of the unthought 'worlding' at work in them, a 'basic meaning' (P: 21) hitherto unacknowledged. There is no quest for some supreme 'name', nor is it a matter of 'the procurement of newly formed words' (WL: 135), but of a transformed relation to language itself.

A POSTCOLONIAL HEIDEGGER?

This brings us to one seemingly obvious option for thought which Heidegger yet rejects. Why not delimit Western thinking by opening a dialogue with the thinking and languages of non-Western civilizations? After all, no one more than Heidegger has criticized at so deep a level the bases of Western thought and life, making him, before the term was even invented, a major thinker of 'globalization'. Given that Western modes of social organization are coming to dominate the whole planet, an engagement with Eastern traditions might seem to offer an irreplaceable resource. The extent of Heidegger's debt to Eastern thought is a matter of continuing debate (see May 1996; Fóti 1998). His knowledge of it seems to have been broad, with an especial interest in the Taoist work of Laotzu, from the sixth century BC (Pet: 168, 181–3). Heidegger's most public engagement, however, is with the Buddhist tradition, in one of his experimental dialogues: 'A Dialogue on Language between a Japanese and an Enquirer' (WL: 1–54). This dialogue seems to arise out of actual encounters between Japanese thinkers and Heidegger. Japanese, or the world of its language, is certainly held to enact modes of being alien to Western productionist metaphysics, so alien in fact, that the Japanese speaker, in dialogue with the 'inquirer' (the Heidegger figure) finds it almost impossible to express them in a Western language like German. The delicate discipline of the dialogue, carefully and patiently undergone, manages to open the smallest crack in the door to a space outside, but this is no sooner glimpsed than it threatens to disappear. Elsewhere Heidegger argues:

> it is my conviction that a reversal can be prepared only in the same place in the world where the modern technological world originated, and that it cannot happen because of any takeover by Zen Buddhism or any other Eastern experiences of the world. . . . Thinking itself can be transformed only by a thinking which has the same origin and calling.

> (Only: 113)

Nevertheless, even if one agrees that Western thought can only be genuinely transformed from within, it is still difficult to agree with the exclusive privilege Heidegger gives in this possible transformation to Germany and the Germans. The supreme relation between languages for Heidegger is that between German and (ancient) Greek. 'Along with German the Greek language is (in regard to the possibilities of thought) at once the most powerful and most spiritual of all languages' (IM: 57). Languages such as English, Latin and French Heidegger saw as deeply impoverished for thought. It is through relation to the deeply alien language of the Greeks, Heidegger argued, that the German language, thought and people might awaken themselves to their deepest possibilities, and to their role of spiritual leadership in Europe.

The best answer to such linguistic nationalism in Heidegger is the very vitality of thinking indebted to him in other languages – Derrida's thinking from out of the resources of French, particularly its syntax (as opposed to Heidegger's focus on individual German words) or the liveliness of English in American Heideggerians like David Krell (Krell 1992).

So we have in Heidegger a strange blend of arguments and stances. He is critical as no one else of a violence inherent at the very bases of Western thought. He is fascinated by encounters with Buddhism and knew intimately the Taoist thinker Laotzu, seeing in both real alternatives to Western tradition. He loathes the United States and keenly supports efforts to resist the encroachment of Western modes of life upon other parts of the globe. He does not believe, however, that engagement with non-Western civilizations is a sufficient option for Western thinkers themselves, whose deepest assumptions can only be shaken from within the largely unthought traditions that determine their existence.

At the same time the alternative modes of life to which Heidegger seems most deeply drawn are European, those of an agrarian, peasant life which was fast disappearing, and which he seems to idealize, as in the essay 'Why Do I Stay in the Provinces?' [1934] (Heidegger 1977b), or the image of peasant shoes he finds in the Van Gogh painting (PLT: 33–4). Even some of Heidegger's prejudices, such as his uncritical patriotism, are those of a fantasy peasant.

HEIDEGGER'S EXPERIMENTS WITH LANGUAGE

It will be obvious by now that Heideggerian thinking questions traditional methods of philosophical argument, and calls for a different kind of practice. One of the most exciting aspects but least recognized of Heidegger's work is his continual experimentation with the generic and formal structures of philosophy as a written practice, deploying new modes of cohesiveness, unity and conclusiveness. Thinking, after Heidegger, cannot be the act of would-be sovereign consciousness seeking the security of an assured and totalizing system of water-tight concepts. This metaphysical picture of thought is memorably caricatured by Heidegger as the securing of 'booty' from the 'outer' world into the stronghold of the mind (BT: 89). Such a mode of knowledge is linked to the instrumentalist and fundamentally aggressive project of Western rationality, now in its globalizing phase. Thinking for Heidegger is not essentially the act of a subjective consciousness positing various representations of an object-world. It must instead be a non-assertive tracing out of the measure and manner of the realm of un-concealment in which it already moves. So it is not a matter of 'grasping', 'securing', 'making certain', and 'mastering' but of 'following', 'hearkening', 'hinting', and 'being guided'. The reductionist process of analysing something into a series of tightly secured separate items must give way to something far less familiar – the opening out, non-appropriatively, to the holistic 'world' presupposed but not recognized by the analytic stance.

The most common form Heidegger deploys is the lecture. Witnesses testify to the dramatic power of his teaching as an oral discipline. Other texts are published as essayistic meditations. The most inventive forms used are the dialogue, as in 'A Dialogue on Language' (WL: 1–54) or 'Conversation on a Country Path' (D: 58–90), and, as in the posthumous *Contributions*, that of the series of note-like passages, some aphoristic, some almost essay-like. This strange experimental text of 1936–8, published only in 1989, is now recognized as Heidegger's greatest work after *Being and Time*, though it is hardly one for the Heideggerian novice (unlike much of the dialogues). A note-like form was also used in different ways by Hölderlin and Nietzsche and by Heidegger's contemporary Wittgenstein in his *Philosophical Investigations* (1953).

In addition to the dialogues and the *Contributions*, there are also various short texts which seem like poems or a poetic sequence but which may only receive due attention once the question of their genre is posed less assuredly. Heidegger called one such sequence 'Hints', denying they should be called poems (GA 13: 23–33). Heidegger writes that these texts, which superficially read like rather poor poems, are not poems, nor versified philosophy. They are the partial coming to word of a thinking that is yet unfulfilled there. A thinking, Heidegger writes, which attempts to think being itself, as opposed to particular beings, cannot rest on sensuous images except as a kind of sheet-anchor for a venture which should ideally be imageless: 'As opposed to the word of poetry the language of thinking is imageless' (GA 13: 33). This means that sequences like 'Hints' [1941], or 'Thoughts' [1971] (for the French poet René Char), or the subtly beautiful 'From out of the Experience of Thinking' [1947] form a unique genre that is yet to be fully recognized. It is one perhaps less akin to most Western poetry than to the terse sayings and work of thought found in a Zen Buddhist Koan – terse, often enigmatic sayings enacting a discipline of mind. Anglophone readers of Heidegger have not been helped by the fact that 'From out of the Experience of Thinking', is available in English under the misleading title 'The Thinker as Poet' (PLT: 1–14).

In this continuous formal experimentation Heidegger, despite his disdain for most modern art and the superficiality of literary criticism, is aligned with 'modernist' and 'post-modernist' projects in various arts and disciplines. For example, Maurice Blanchot's avant-garde narrative, *L'attente L'oubli* (1962) reuses text from a Heideggerian-type dialogue, 'L'attente'(Blanchot 1959), which Blanchot had first released for the *Festschrift* for Heidegger's seventieth birthday in 1959.

Heidegger's experiments strive to practise a non-representational thinking. How then can Heidegger proceed to study the essence of language? He cannot take the normal route of assuming language to be an object like any other, then go on to distinguish and classify its various parts and the rules that seem to govern their interrelationships. Language cannot be studied, as linguistics does, by evading the question of its mode of being. Nor can we step outside language, for human beings always find themselves in language and the world it opens. To imagine not having language is as impossible as imagining having nothing to imagine with. There is no way to language except as a path that turns back upon itself, transforming itself as it does so. The aim must be to avoid merely writing *about* language but 'to bring language to language as language' (WL: 113; trans. modified). Wittgenstein argued similarly: 'What is spoken can only be explained in language and so in this sense language cannot be explained. Language must speak for itself' (Wittgenstein 1974b: 40).

The thinker must take a *step back* from language, that is to give it the kind of non-coercive, presuppositionless attention we have already seen at work in relation to the lectern in the first chapter or the temple and painting in the third. It means not presupposing that we already know its mode of being and then trying to get a clearer concept of it as if it were an object one could turn at every angle beneath our eyes. Released from such attitudes thought may become attentive to the delicate but all-powerful way in which language articulates the open space or clearing in which we find ourselves, making things accessible with the significances and implications that give them their determinate being. It brings things to a world and a world to things.

The 'poems', the dialogues and much of the *Contributions* cannot be read as being 'about' something in the familiar sense of making a conceptual model of it. They strive towards the status of a thinking-in-action. Such an awareness is approached, surprisingly, by a close attention to the failings of language, those places where the language received from tradition breaks down. Failure here means not just the lack or the inadequacy of a particular expression or term, but, as in the issue of translation, those moments in which the adequacy of a language as a whole is at issue. This is where, losing our seeming control of language, something of its power emerges. In the *Contributions* we read:

> The word fails, not as an occasional event – in which an accomplishable speech or expression does not take place, where only the assertion and the repetition of something already said and sayable does not get accomplished – but originarily [i.e. it is language as a whole that fails, not just the lack of a specific word]. The word does not even come to word, even though it is precisely when the word escapes one that the word begins to take its first leap.

> (C: 26)

No wonder, perhaps, that the *Contributions* are a series of halting notes. The title itself, with its studied banality, advertises its own stand-in status. The gaps, the seeming repetitions of the ventures of thought, the dryings up into staccato notes, all bespeak the necessity of a certain failure as part of whatever success this thought may achieve. Heidegger's writing is marked by pauses, spacing and the use of lineation to draw thinking into the pull of the unthought.

The dialogues are if anything more inventive. Heidegger seems to have been especially drawn to this form in the crisis years of the mid-1940s (GA 77). Often they do not dramatize arguments in which one speaker tries to prove his or her view right and the others wrong. They make up a shared listening to language in the halting, non-competitive to and fro of meditative exchange. The *dramatis personae* are less characters than places for the momentary failure, pause and enforced listening of thinking to language. Thus in 'Conversation on a Country Path' (D: 58–90) the possibility of a non-representational, non-objectifying thinking is at work both as a topic and as the putative medium or path followed by three minimally characterized speakers, named to suggest slightly differing attitudes to the nature of thought:

Scholar: Probably it can't be re-presented at all, in so far as in re-presenting everything has become an object that stands opposite us within a horizon.

Scientist: Then we can't really describe what we have named?

Teacher: No. Any description would reify it.

Scholar: Nevertheless it lets itself be named, and being named it can be thought about . . .

Teacher:	. . . only if thinking is no longer re-presenting.
Scientist:	But then what else should it be?
Teacher:	Perhaps we now are close to being released into the nature of thinking . . .
Scholar:	. . . through waiting for its nature.

(D: 67)

Passages like this enact a virtuosity of thinking still to be fully recognized. The failure of language in re-presentation here is not simply the loss of all means to think further. Rather, that failure is itself the process whereby the new mode of thinking opens up, the one described here (provisionally) as a 'waiting'. Such thinking is no longer the positing of various representations of an object–world. Instead, thought must also turn back upon itself, attentive to the contours of its own existence, but without thereby posing itself as a self-certain consciousness against which an object–thing is posited. Thought turns upon itself as the question of its own nature and that nature is, correlatively, the open space of such a turning and questioning. It is such a space for thinking, not an object thought, which the dialogue opens out with its faltering movements of pause and restart. This Heidegger terms 'releasement' (*Gelassenheit*).

Heidegger's practice aligns him with the post- or anti-modernist practice of writers such as Samuel Beckett or Blanchot, with their persistent refusal of formal or conceptual closure, as opposed to the kinds of aesthetic autonomy at work in high modernist works by Ezra Pound and T. S. Eliot with their stress on spatial form, mythic analogy and epiphanic climax. Heidegger deploys fragmentation, provisional or incomplete structures not by vague analogy to the supposed chaos of the world, but as part of an ascetic discipline in which thought is defamiliarized and transformed by an encounter with its own borders.

Likewise, as we shall see in the next chapter, the essential nature of the poetic was revealed for Friedrich Hölderlin, the supreme poet for Heidegger, from out of the very failure of poetry to achieve itself fully in modern Europe (hence Hölderlin is seen as the poet of the nature of poetry).

SUMMARY

This chapter has ranged through various issues all relating to Heidegger's distinctive take on language.

Heidegger rejects the received, common-sense view that language is primarily a tool of human communication. This view is superficial, he argues, because it presupposes the deeper way in which language, even as we speak, already forms a kind of all-pervading environment, making things articulable for us in a world in the first place.

As such a primary environment, language is the bearer of deep history in the sense of that 'obvious' sense of things in which people have lived in various epochs. Any freeing of our ourselves from the burden of productionist metaphysics must involve a radical defamiliarizing of the language that carries it, including ordinary language, however seemingly devoid of philosophical assumptions it may at first seem.

The commonplace language of today bears down on us with the whole dead weight of metaphysical tradition. At the same time language is also the supreme resource for Heidegger's thinking. His work consists mainly of revisionist readings of the crucial texts of the Western tradition. He reads against the letter, attentive to the kind of *unthought* world out of which the text arose, whether its author was explicitly conscious of this or not, and he employs a variety of defamiliarizing strategies to open the word up, with a view to reawakening the whole way of life at work in or vehicled by the language. These strategies include the consideration of various possible translations, attention to etymologies, to related words and their associations and history. In this way, instead of the traditional philosophical procedure of reducing language to the status of being the tool of discrete and unequivocal concepts, expressing supposedly timeless 'problems', Heidegger opens out the language of his text to revive a sense of the deepest, implicit but all-pervasive assumptions and modes of being inherent in it – the unreflective sense of things which both makes possible yet is denied by productionist metaphysics.

Finally, we turned to the way in which Heidegger's rejection of the instrumentalist conception of language led to his various provisional experiments with new modes of writing and practicing philosophy. These included his use of the dialogue form, his seeming 'poems' and the posthumously published *Contributions* (*Beiträge*). *Wege nicht Werke*, 'ways not works', was Heidegger's choice as the motto for his collected works.

QUIZZICAL INTERLUDE

What *is* a literary work?

You may like to know about an intellectual conjuring trick that proves, or seems to prove, that a literary work does not exist. You take various plausible ideas as to what sort of thing a given work is, and then show with one or two simple arguments that it cannot be anything of the sort. Finally, as various ideas as to its mode of being are exhausted, the work seems to have been proved not to exist.

Let us take *Hamlet* again. First, we might want to say *Hamlet* exists in the same way as does the *Mona Lisa* or the *Parthenon*, also great works of art. This means that one is saying that just as the *Mona Lisa* exists as a physical object, currently located in France, or as the Parthenon exists in Athens (mostly), so *Hamlet* too is a unique physical object. Yet this would be obviously wrong. If the original copy of *Hamlet* is destroyed, the play is not destroyed as long as accurate copies remain. On the other hand, if we destroy an artefact such as the *Parthenon*, we destroy it completely, as imitations will be regarded as having a lesser status than the original. Finally, even if one did accept the hypothesis that *Hamlet* is essentially some early seventeenth-century object, there would be further problems: for instance the printed page contains many elements which still seem extraneous or accidental in relation to the literary work, such as the page size used or the kind of typeface.

The work, then, is not a material thing. So one might want to say that it is only really there when performed. *Hamlet,* in that case, *is* the sounds and actions of the actors, or correspondingly, the internal vocal-ization that is the performance of silent reading. This seems plausible at first but is easily refuted. If a work is the same as its performance does this not make each different production or reading a separate work? Two readings of *Hamlet* would not be two different realizations of the *same* work, but distinct works. At the same time any one perfor-mance may realize only some aspects of the work, leaving others latent and perhaps to be made explicit in other performances. After all, we distinguish good and bad performances of a work and this clearly assumes that the work and the performance are not identical things.

A third try. A commonsense answer to the dilemma now suggests itself. We say 'yes, such a such an interpretation is fine, but what was in Shakespeare's mind etc.?' We identify the work with the author's plans and intentions in writing. Yet, the assumption that the reader's job is to get at 'what the author meant' is indefensible if this is taken as some original intending or mental thing or act present at the time of writing. For most writers no evidence whatever survives of such circumstances. In any case, even if we had perfect evidence as to Shakespeare's mental state while writing *Hamlet*, this would surely be treated as evidence towards an interpretation of the work, not as the real thing.

A fourth and final answer to the dilemma – what is the mode of being of the literary work of art? – brings us to the assumption at work in much contemporary academic writing. The real work is the work as it appeared to readers at the time of its initial publication. Thus the real nature of the text, it is argued, can be reconstructed only by minute historical research into the social and political context in which it artic-ulated itself. This is the answer implicit in the forms of *historicism* now dominant in criticism. Yet again an objection springs to mind, espe-cially if one is at a salutary distance from a university. Are people really still going to see *Hamlet* out of a deep interest in English or in Danish history? Do we really read Goethe, say, only to learn about his histor-ical epoch? Does this not suggest that the work is not simply a historical document in the received sense? Furthermore, if the arguments of this sort of historicism are accepted, can we really assume that the play ever meant the same thing to diverse people and interests even when it first was seen, i.e. that there was ever one original 'real' *Hamlet*? And then even if the 'true' *Hamlet* is that which was apparent to the early seventeenth century, can this really mean that subsequent readings (e.g. in terms of psychoanalytic notions such as the Oedipus complex) must be invalid? A quote from Heidegger can be brought in here, anticipating the argument with such historicism in his thought. The quotidian understanding of history will not accept, he writes,

> that Sophocles ... [and] Kant one day can and must be interpreted differently. . . . But the conventional view is that there is such a thing as a Sophocles in itself or a Kant in itself . . . just as that table there is a table and that pencil a pencil. Suppose for instance there could be an explanation and representation of the poetry of Sophocles in itself and that it fell under the eyes of Sophocles, he could only find this interpretation utterly boring.

> (GA 39: 145)

Heidegger's interest, as we will further explore (Chapter 6), is not in the work as an historical object, but rather in its relation to deep history (*Geschichte*), its continuing engagement with major questions in human existence, with assumptions which change only rarely over the centuries.

In sum, it would seem that a literary text can be identified neither simply as a material object, nor as a psychological object experienced by a reader or readers, nor identified with its author's original intentions and nor, finally, with the work as it appeared in its original historical context. What space is left? Have we really proved that *Hamlet* does not exist?

Or rather have we not proved Heidegger's point that the work does not have the mode of being of an object present-at-hand in any sense, either material, psychological or social?

The argument given here is not particularly profound (in fact, as given so far, it might apply to any work of language). However, it does suggest the philosophical naiveté of most assumptions about the nature of the work even in professional criticism. It clears a space in which to turn to further Heidegger's extraordinary and sometimes counterintuitive readings of poetry.

6

HEIDEGGER AND THE POETIC

Behind the technological world there is a mystery. This world is not just a creation of human beings. No one knows whether and when humans will ever experience this emptiness as the 'sacred empty'. It suffices that this relation remains open.

(Letter to Ingeborg Böttger, 25 February 1968: Pet: 61)

A person who reads Heidegger and the monumental issues in his texts interested only in extracting some new method of reading to be added to the stockpile of literary criticism – this might be a good definition of an idiot. Heidegger's readings of poets have been widely if often implicitly influential, but they were never in fact primarily intended as part of the business of literary criticism, a discipline Heidegger saw as a parochial representative of the sort of thinking he was trying to challenge. A disclaimer added to the fourth edition of Heidegger's study of Hölderlin (1971) reads: 'The present *Elucidations* do not aim to be contributions to research in the history of literature or to aesthetics. They spring from a necessity of thought' (E: 21). That necessity relates to Heidegger's discovery, in certain poetic texts, of modes of thought and being that offer a radical alternative to productionist thinking and the world of techno-science. Heidegger's engagement with the poetic, especially the work of Friedrich Hölderlin, is the subject of this chapter.

FRIEDRICH HÖLDERLIN

In 1914 Heidegger writes, an 'earthquake' hit him (WL: 78). He means not the outbreak of World War but his reading of the extraordinary Romantic poet, Friedrich Hölderlin (1770–1843). Heidegger encountered Hölderlin in the historic first edition of Norbert von Hellingrath, published seven decades after the poet's death in 1843, and more than a hundred after his eclipse by insanity in 1806. He stated that 'My thinking stands in an unavoidable relationship to the poetry of Hölderlin' (Only: 122). The poets R. M. Rilke (PLT: 91–142) and Stefan George (1868–1933) (WL: 139–58) are the subject of a published lecture each by Heidegger, Georg Trakl (1887–1914) of two (PLT: 189–210: WL: 159–98), Hölderlin is the subject of ten. These include a book, *Elucidations of Hölderlin's Poetry* first published in 1944 and re-issued in expanded editions up to 1971. A large amount of new material has recently been published (GA 75 (2000)). In 1963, introducing a recording made of him reading ten Hölderlin texts, Heidegger re-affirmed, his voice shrill with age, that 'Hölderlin's poetry is a fate for us' (E: 224). 'He calls out toward the turning of time' (E: 226).

Heidegger's work on the poetic has been immensely influential, but not on the surface. It is contrary to the spirit of Heidegger's thinking that it should found any school or be schematized into a technics of interpretation. Gerald Bruns goes so far as to say that there is no 'cash value' of Heidegger's thinking on the poetic, nothing, that is, which a student of literary or cultural theory could simply take away and apply elsewhere (Bruns 1989: xxv). This is an exaggeration, I think. However, it is fair to say of Heidegger's interpretations of Hölderlin what is perhaps true of his thought generally: that those aspects of it that function as a deconstruction of traditional thinking have been lastingly influential, whereas Heidegger's more 'positive' elaboration of new ways of hearkening to being have had less effect and been criticized. For instance, I know of no living critic who would endorse the peculiarly exalted importance that Heidegger gives Hölderlin, let alone the redemptive nationalist politics at work in some of the readings. My focus in this chapter, then, will be on the kinds of questioning in Heidegger's lectures that remain to engage us.

Hölderlin bears the weight of all that Heidegger is trying to find redemptive in art. His work had first turned to Hölderlin in the winter semester of 1934–5, in the aftermath of the debacle of his failed engagement in politics. He was to give lectures on Hölderlin for decades afterwards, widening his frame of reference from the crisis being undergone by Germany to that of the modern West as a whole.

The reception of Heidegger's readings of poetry has been held back by a simplistic understanding of Heidegger's affirmation of Hölderlin's view that poets are the real founders and determiners of human history, legislating the basic myths, assumptions and ways of seeing that are then inhabited by others. As we saw in Chapter 3, such an ideal of art is one to which Heidegger aspired (as did Hölderlin): for both however, theirs is a time of the possible death of art under the dominance of technological and objectifying ways of life. The whole point of Heidegger's turning to poetry is to do justice to modes of being and thinking that are still not fully determined by productionist metaphysics. So Heidegger's claim is hardly that Hölderlin's work already founds a new historical epoch. The issue is to help let the work 'happen' as part of such a beginning. There is sometimes a messianic quality in these texts: 'It may be that one day we shall have to move out of our everydayness and move into the power of poetry, that we shall never again return into everydayness as we left it' (GA 39: 22).

No one gives Hölderlin more decisive status than Heidegger. The main reason is the force of the poetry, the concern of most of this chapter. Hölderlin is also decisive for two further reasons. First, Hölderlin's work arises out of an engagement with one great highpoint of German and Western philosophy, 'German Idealism' in the form of the work of G. W. F. Hegel (1770–1831), F. W. J. Schelling (1775–1854) and J. G. Fichte (1762–1814) (the former two had been fellow seminary students with Hölderlin). For Heidegger, Hölderlin's questioning proximity to German idealist philosophy gives his work the singular status of being other than metaphysical thinking in a way that directly feeds into Heideggerian *Destruction*. So symbiotic becomes the relationship between Hölderlin and Heidegger that Heidegger's later thought deploys many of Hölderlin's own terms. For instance the later Heidegger further elaborates his dichotomy of 'earth' and 'world' into a 'fourfold', derived from Hölderlin, of 'mortals', 'earth', 'sky' and 'divinities' (e.g. PLT: 165–86). The second contextual reason for Hölderlin's decisiveness is that his poetry and thought is in dialogue with the Greek beginnings of Western thought, a dialogue so profound that Heidegger sees Hölderlin alone among the great thinkers and writers of this time, including even J. W. von Goethe (1749–1832), as offering the possibility of a genuine rethinking of the basic elements of Western destiny.

WHAT IS A HEIDEGGERIAN READING? BASIC FEATURES

First of all, as should be clear from the last brief section ('Quizzical Interlude'), the literary work is not an object in a familiar way, i.e. not something that is simply there and available for study as a tree or a window would be. The reader will already miss what concerns Heidegger in the poetic if he or she approaches the work as an *object* of possible knowledge in the usual way, that is as something which can be scanned by detached consciousness from the outside, its parts itemized as so many 'word things' with a view to their 'unity' or lack of it, or studied for its place in a taxonomy of genres or to be situated in the movements of cultural history. Heidegger's goal is a transformation of the reader's deepest assumptions: most approaches in literary study, in other words, must be left behind.

So one must not think of Heidegger's approach to the poetic in terms of what are usually called 'problems of criticism', issues such as the place of an author's intention in determining meaning, the correctness or otherwise of an interpretation, the cultural politics of the aesthetic etc. It is not that Heidegger's work does not have implications for all of these issues, but that his thinking would avoid addressing its matter as a 'problem' in the first place. This may seem counterintuitive, but the very concept of something as a problem is a part of a technicist thinking that tackles its object in an instrumentalist resultsoriented manner. The jargon of 'problem' pervades and structures modern life and the media, posing every kind of issue – human rights, the economy, the environment, education – as a 'problem' to be fixed.

To highlight his distance from the compromised sub-discipline of literary criticism, Heidegger draws a further distinction, calling the work which engages him '*Dichtung*' or 'poetry', as opposed to 'literature', which he usually dismisses. By 'literature' he means those works which merely relate to the values and issues of their immediate historical (*historische*) context: there 'the validity of literature is assessed by the latest prevailing standard. The prevailing standard, in turn, is made and controlled by the organs for making public civilized opinions' (PLT: 213–14). Among such organs would be the education system and the institution of criticism, whose powers are reductive: 'In such a setting poetry [*Dichtung*] cannot appear otherwise than as literature' (PLT: 214).

Dichtung then, if is to be preserved in its singular force, must be distinguished and removed from the familiar arena of conflicting values and interests that make up the institutions of literature and criticism. It is something else entirely, of an elusive and easily occluded mode of being.

What then is *Dichtung*?

The German term is not fully equivalent to the English 'poetry'. It means imaginative literature in general, and not just verse – for instance Heidegger would include Joseph Conrad's prose as genuine *Dichtung* (Pet: 196). Simply put, *Dichtung* in Heidegger is a strongly evaluative term, naming a work of language which has all the features of a genuine work of art as described in Chapter 3. There too we already saw Heidegger's conviction that most official or professional reception of art was effectively its suffocation.

NOT READING FOR THE 'CONTENT'

This issue brings us back to a crucial feature of the art work, its singularity. The poetic work (*Dichtung*), in its resistant, 'self-sufficient presence' (PLT: 29), is not reducible to what a reader already understands. It brings into existence something new that needs to be understood only in its own terms: "The truth that discloses itself in the work can never be proved or derived from what went before. What went before is refuted in its exclusive reality by the work' (PLT: 75).

This leads to the most notable feature of Heidegger's readings. To affirm the singularity of the poetic is necessarily to affirm the singularity of any reading which responds to it. The resistance of Heidegger's texts here is that he refuses to 'decode' the singularity of the text into some general 'content' or nascent system of thought but deploys and rests upon the words and images of the text at issue. His procedure is usually to home in relentlessly on certain crucial terms in the text (as we have seen him do with *logos* in Heraclitus) then open them up by all the strategies of internal translation and defamiliarization described in the last chapter. Thus the readings of Friedrich Hölderlin remain couched in

Hölderlin's own terms of 'the unknown god', 'the holy' and 'the home-land' and that of Georg Trakl in Trakl's terms of 'the stranger', 'spirit', 'blue' and so on. As 'The Origin of the Work of Art' reminds us: 'Where does the work belong? The work belongs, as work, uniquely within the realm that is opened up by itself' (PLT: 41). Heidegger's internal trans-lating tries to carry us towards that point at which the poetic words would become no longer just objects of our thinking but that *through* which we think, without need of paraphrase, so delivering us over to the unique realm opened in the poetry. '[T]he elucidating speech must each time shatter itself and what it had attempted to do' and 'the most diffi-cult step of every interpretation . . . consists in its disappearing before the pure presence of the poem' (E: 22). It is of course an asymptotic or finally impossible ideal and, needless to say, Heidegger has been argued to stand in the way of the pure self-presencing of the poems in various ways (see Chapter 7, pp. 128–32), and the ideal itself criticized (Chapter 8, pp. 152–3). This resistant proximity to the very letter of the text ren-ders Heidegger's readings only partly generalizable into some transfer-able mode of reading.

As we saw at the opening of this study, Heidegger's pervading con-cern is to challenge what 'knowledge' usually means, diagnosing and repudiating the reductive violence implicit in the kinds of knowledge that have become dominant in the West, with their vocabulary of 'mastering', 'conquering', 'grasping', 'making certain' and so on. A reading that respects the irreducible singularity of the text is moving towards the practice of non-appropriative knowing. For instance, in Heidegger's reading of Hölderlin's 'Wie wenn am Feiertag' (written 1800) Heidegger's way is to focus on the key word 'Nature' and its cognates in that poetic fragment. He cannot assume that this term can be understood simply by reference to what 'Nature' means in, say, the natural philosophy or the religion of Hölderlin's time, an approach that would close off in advance the possibility that the text might be doing something singular and new. Instead, Heidegger utilizes the strategies of internal translation discussed in the previous chapter to ease out the precise inflection which the term is given in Hölderlin's work: 'what this word 'nature', known since long ago and long since worn out in its ambiguity, is to signify here must be determined solely out of this single poem' (E: 78). Thus 'Nature' takes on a singular force, unique to Hölderlin, one no longer identifiable with what 'Nature' means or meant in given systems of religion or philosophy.

The same procedure applies to a key phrase in Hölderlin's œuvre, 'the gods': Heidegger writes:

> instead of reading the works of poets and thinkers, it has become the custom merely to read books 'about' them, or even excerpts from such books, there is the even more acute danger of the opinion setting in that the gods in Hölderlin's poetry could be ascertained and discussed via literary [i.e. literary historical] means. It makes no essential difference whether one also calls upon Christian theology for assistance and expounds the view that Hölderlin's doctrine concerning the gods is a fallen version of the one, true Christian monotheism, or whether one 'explains' these gods with the aid of Greek mythology and its Roman variations.

(Ist: 32)

(We will return to 'the gods' shortly.) Heidegger demands that we leave behind that familiar kind of reading that tries to extract some kind of philosophical or religious 'content' from out of the texture of poetizing. Such a mode of critical attention, seemingly so reasonable, would destroy in advance the possibility of hearkening to what is essential and singular in the poetic.

CONTEXT?

Another crucial issue in 'The Origin of the Work of Art', let us recall, was the rejection of the notion that art is a reflection or mirror of some sort. The true work of art does not simply take things or objects already in existence and then re-present them, as in the tired old view of art as a sort of 'reflection' of reality or society. Instead of merely re-presenting what is already apparent, the poetic engages and can change the most basic sense of things, the overall context or 'world' in which things are apparent to us in the first place. Hubert Dreyfus gives a helpful example. He writes of the poetic in terms of what he calls 'background practices':

> an artist or a thinker, just like anyone else, cannot be clear about the background practices of his life and his age, not just because there are so many of them that such explication is an infinite task, but because the background is not a set of assumptions or beliefs about which one could even in principle be clear. .... This is what Heidegger calls the essential unthought in the work.

> The greater the work of a thinker ... the richer is the unthought in the work, i.e. that which through that work and through it alone, comes up as never-yet-thought.
>
> As this passage implies, this unthought is not at some unsoundable depth but right upon the surface. It can best be noticed in the case of thinkers whose intuitive grasp extends beyond that of their contemporaries (e.g. Melville in *Moby Dick*). ... We cannot speak of *the* meaning of a work ... because there is no final determinate meaning to get at.
>
> (Dreyfus 1985: 236–7)

Dreyfus's reading helps us by relating Heidegger to that vague but strong sense that in literature is put into language as nowhere else a general 'spirit of the age', the fundamental quiddity of a time or place. That granted, one must remember that Heidegger is not talking of the accidents of either individual or social psychology, but deep history, the fundamental attitudes that determine a whole civilization, the 'history of being'.

For Heidegger then, approaching a poem by Hölderlin or Trakl, the 'context' at issue is not primarily something the critic is supposed to reconstruct with a view to fixing some ideal of what the text 'originally meant' within that context. With *Dichtung,* things are the other way round, i.e. the poetic text reveals the context which might have been held to explain it – 'the pervasive individual and social self-interpretation [the] work embodies' (Dreyfus 1985, 236–7) – making this newly perceptible and questionable.

What does this mean in Hölderlin's case? For Heidegger, Hölderlin's work, with its concern with spiritual destitution, longing, and national crisis, reveals the modern condition as one which Heidegger would term *nihilism*. The world prevailing but usually unrecognized in the language of his (and Heidegger's) time becomes legible: that of the triumph of instrumentalist reason, the objectification of the environment, the lack of 'the gods' in Hölderlin's idiom.

Heidegger's and Hölderlin's concern is to address what other thinkers, after the sociologist Max Weber (1864–1920) call the 'disenchantment' of the world in modernity (see Cascardi 1992: 16–71). The 'lack of God' defining our era is not a denial that 'the Christian relationship with God lives on in individuals and in the churches' (PLT: 91), but is a recognition that religion has long lost its world-historical significance. It is not a matter of a belief in this or that divinity, but the loss and oblivion, in the era's prevailing conceptions of reality and humanity, of the whole dimension in which such questions arise except, meaninglessly, as a kind of life-style choice: 'It has already grown so destitute, it can no longer discern the default of God as a default' (PLT: 91).

Hölderlin is the poet of fundamental spiritual crisis, of our time as a destitute time of waiting, a meanwhile that cannot be measured but only endured. His odes, modelled in a peculiarly Greek German on those of Pindar more than two millennia ago, enact what might be termed a religion without an object. In this way Hölderlin has been seen to trace the boundaries of modern European existence. Blanchot writes of Hölderlin in terms that align him with twentieth-century writers such as himself and Samuel Beckett:

> in a present that was null, companionless, having nothing to say and nothing to do except this very nothing, [Hölderlin] was deeply aware of existing only in waiting, in movement held above its nothingness.
>
> (Blanchot 1982a: 117)

Hölderlin's phrase 'the gods' is singular in standing mainly for a lack, almost as a cipher marking a space that might one day be filled, and not a name whose originals might be pointed out.

'POETRY OF POETRY'

The distinctiveness of Hölderlin for Heidegger is not, however, that he writes *about* such nihilism, but that his poetry is itself a mode of language that engages it by enacting the possibility of other non-appropriative ways of knowing. Heidegger writes that Hölderlin's is a 'poetry of poetry' (E: 52). He means by this not some vague notion of poetry which is about itself, becoming a sort of criticism, but poetry engaged explicitly with the very kind of disclosive power described in 'The Origin of the Work of Art', in other words with its power of revealing deep history (*Geschichte*), those most basic and unthought modes of being which are normally too close, or too obvious, for us to see. For instance, one of the most immediately powerful and unusually celebratory of Hölderlin's poems is 'Homecoming' (1802). Here the poem concerns the occasion of the poet's return home, to his native land, travelling across a lake to a small southern German town shadowed by the Alps. 'All seems familiar, even the hurried greetings / Seem those of friends, every face seems a kindred one' (E: 27). Everything, in the homecoming, is familiar but estranged by being seen anew, newly realized in its specific nature in a way imperceptible to a daily inhabitant who has never left and to whom all is unproblematically ordinary. To bring the familiar nearer by perceiving at a new distance, to cherish what we recognize by acknowledging the resistance of its otherness, this is the force of the poetic which Heidegger celebrates in this, one of Hölderlin's happiest texts.

So, what does it mean to see this as a 'poetry of poetry'? The poem is clearly about the nature and duty of the poet, but that is only superficially the issue. For Heidegger, after Hölderlin's own poetics and practice, the *act* of the poem itself, in the time of its being read, is itself such a homecoming in process:

> Homecoming is not a poem about homecoming; rather, the elegy, the poetic activity which it is, is the homecoming itself, and still it comes to pass as long as its words ring like a bell in the language of the German people.

> (E: 44)

The kind of poetic perception engaged in 'Homecoming' corresponds to Hölderlin's own concept of a true 'intimacy' (*Innigkeit*) with things or people. This alternative notion of knowing is not, of course, just a matter of the subjective feelings of the returned traveller, though that may be provisionally helpful as an analogue: it involves Hölderlin's deepest engagement with the unregarded assumptions and modes of perception of his age, with what would later be termed nihilism. This 'intimacy' is the notion (surely in debate with the model of knowledge being elaborated at this time by Hölderlin's friend Hegel (GA 39: 129ff)) of a 'poetic' knowing that brings nearer but by allowing distance, joins together by acknowledging separateness and 'understands' in yet holding a reserve of the non-intelligible (see GA 39: 249–50). This is what Heidegger's lecture calls the 'mystery of the reserving nearness' (E: 43, 47), or simply, the 'sacred' (E: 46). These polarities in the 'sacred' (of near and far, understanding and mystery) are contradictions which for Hölderlin it is the force of the poetic to hold and sustain, rather than demanding their further resolution by reason. Here is the basis of Heidegger's affirmation of the poetic as a kind of alternative non-reductive knowledge:

The poet knows that when he calls the reserved 'the real find', that is, something he has found, he says something that runs counter to common sense. To say that something is near while it remains distant means, after all, violating a fundamental principle of ordinary thought, the principle of contradiction, or else playing with empty words, or else making an outrageous statement. That is why the poet, almost as soon as he has brought himself to say his words about the mystery of the reserving nearness, interrupts himself:

I talk like a fool.

But he talks nevertheless. The poet must talk, for

It is joy.

(E: 43)

As 'Homecoming' shows us, by 'poetry of poetry' is not meant some sort of reflexive text that spirals in upon itself, but one that opens outwards upon the most basic traits of its time and place – disenchantment and the need for the 'sacred' in Hölderlin's sophisticated sense of the word. 'Poetry of poetry' is the opposite of an arid kind of navel gazing.

This helps us understand why Hölderlin, for Heidegger, is so special. Heidegger does not deny that in Virgil, Shakespeare, Sophocles or Dante 'the essence of poetry comes to rich expression', more than in Hölderlin (E: 52). Hölderlin's distinctiveness is 'his whole poetic mission', which is 'to make poems solely out of the essence of poetry'. In Hölderlin's 'poetry of poetry', the disclosive, defamiliarizing power of the poetic loses its imperceptibility and becomes itself the issue. Hölderlin turns poetic language back upon its own founding power – his mission is to disclose and affirm this power of sacred disclosure, to poetize poetizing, or to bring the power of language itself to word. This is not an infinite regress but something as elusive and yet fundamental as trying to see, not any thing, but sight itself. It is to render strange by rendering apparent the very obviousness of the obvious. Yet, in 'Homecoming' the poet, unlike the other inhabitants, remains at the end burdened with care as a result of his broader perspective, which embraces the lack of this 'sacred' dimension in the lives of his countrymen, and the continuing weakness of poetry in such an environment to articulate and communicate it.

THE TIME OF THE POEM

Unlike mere 'literature', *Dichtung* cannot justly be approached as a historical document, its details tidily resituated within the debates of its time. The poetic text is historical in its mode of being for Heidegger but in accordance with a very different and profounder understanding of historicity than other forms of historicism. The focus, relentlessly, is on deep history, *Geschichte*, on 'context' in its deepest and most far-reaching sense. We cannot assume the work to be an object that was once a thing in itself and which is now simply present in front of us to be reconstructed. A Hölderlin poem has a date of composition and a historical context, but the deep history (*Geschichte*) it engages, that of European nihilism, is absolutely contemporary. This leads to a thought-provoking consequence: that Heidegger sees Hölderlin as lying in our future at least as much as in our past, exceeding all the critical methods that have hitherto been applied to him or which exist in our time, for these are pervaded by the objectifying assumptions of productionist metaphysics. Hölderlin's work stands within history – the German lands in the period of the French Revolution – but also beside it in the sense of opening a space in which it may yet be decided what 'history' means:

> This essence of poetry belongs to a definite time. But not in such a way that it merely conforms to that time as some time already existing. Rather, by providing anew the essence of poetry, Hölderlin first determines a new time. It is the time of the gods who have fled *and* of the god who is coming.
>
> (E: 64)

If Hölderlin's poems have not yet found their time and space, how is one to approach them? Clearly not simply by reading Hölderlin as a historical figure who wrote at the time of the French Revolution and then lost his mind. Heidegger's approach is not a reading in terms of historical context, nor the elaboration of some sort of 'content', nor a formal analysis of the linguistic and other structures of the text, nor an evaluation. All these familiar modes render the poem a totalized object laid out before the critic. The elucidations are not interpretations aiming at a set of results about the poems. If any kind of event is to transpire in the encounter with the text, we must avoid submitting Hölderlin to the measures of our time, but submit ourselves, but not thoughtlessly, to the measure of the poet. The transformation of the reader is the issue.

HISTORICISM

Historicism, currently very powerful in the literary academy, is definable as 'a critical movement insisting on the prime importance of historical context to the interpretation of texts of all kinds' (Hamilton 1996: 2). The text is understood as an historical document. It belongs 'back there': its understanding is the reconstitution of the precise contexts in which it was embedded or in which it intervened. The more detailed these contexts, the more thoroughly historicized the text and – for the historicist – the better the interpretation. So, oddly, one might object, the more 'topical' the text can be argued to be, the more valuable and interesting it is somehow supposed to become?

In practice, 'historical accuracy' is often be invoked by critics anxious to condemn less orthodox kinds of interpretation. To a Heideggerian, concerned to open up the text in relation to the largest and most pressing questions about human existence, even the partially historicizing rubric for this Routledge Critical Thinkers Series sounds familiarly oppressive. Does not the assurance about placing 'key thinkers firmly back in their context' also sound like a police clamp down?

Heidegger's concerns are thoroughly historical in a sense, but his concern is deep history in the sense of *Geschichte*. Thus, from a Heideggerian viewpoint, traditional historicism does not go deep enough, but works within all kinds of philosophical assumptions that are themselves fundamentally 'historical' in ways that are not acknowledged. As we saw in Chapter 2, Heidegger associates traditional historiography with the 'principle of reason' that governs our epoch of techno-science (QCT: 126–7; Chapter 2, p. 35)

Heidegger writes of the early twentieth-century German poet, Georg Trakl:

> It has been said that Trakl's work is 'profoundly unhistorical.' In this judgment, what is meant by 'history'? If the word means no more than 'chronicle', that is, the rehearsal of past events, then Trakl is indeed unhistorical. His poetry has no need of historical 'objects'. Why not? Because his poetic work is historical in the highest sense. His poetry sings of the destiny which casts humankind forward into its still withheld nature, thereby saving or salvaging the latter.
>
> ('Language in the Poem,' (WL: 196; trans. modified))

The reading must be, from the point of received procedures, an anti-reading.

HEIDEGGER READING HÖLDERLIN'S 'GERMANIA'

I will turn then to the earliest of Heidegger's readings of Hölderlin, the 1934 lectures on the ode 'Germania' ('Germanien' (Hölderlin 1980: 400–7)). Amidst the fascist triumphalism of 1934, Heidegger's first lecture on Hölderlin's ode 'Germania' concerns the way that poem engages the sense of a deep mourning for the withdrawal of 'the gods', yet at the same time it holds open, by its very nature as mourning, a space for a possible new advent.

THE INVOCATION: LANGUAGE AS ACTION

The poem opens with a strangely negative gesture. Hölderlin does not offer a traditional invocation to the muses or to the classical gods, in homage or for inspiration. He opens with the renunciation of such a beginning, as if to marking that an old and familiar kind of poetry is no longer possible:

> Not them, the blessed, who once appeared,
> Those images of gods in the ancient land,
> Them, it is true, I may not now invoke . . .

Yet, this renunciation of invoking is not a simple rejection or dismissal of the gods. It arises from a sense of painful necessity: who can invoke the dead? It does not mean there is no desire for such an invocation. The poem opens itself in the space of an invocation that is longed for but must now be renounced ('I am afraid, for deadly / And scarcely permitted it is to awaken the dead'). So in effect, the non-invocation is formally still a kind of invocation: that is, it remains something whereby the poem opens itself to the space of 'the gods', but it does so in way that bears out how that phrase now stands for a lack only, a cipher marking an empty space that might one day be filled but which for the present can only be kept open, safeguarded from obliteration. That is why the mourning remains a 'sacred' mourning. We are torn, Heidegger writes, between 'the open welcome of readiness' and 'the absence of fulfillment'. What is invoked in not being invoked can have no name in this 'godless' time. It is simply 'the invoked' or 'the awaited' (*das Erharrte*). Any sense of the sacred can no longer look to old gods to be sustained. It is the duty of the poet not to evade this disenchantment. To genuinely hold open the space of the sacred we must think through and endure its current emptiness and destitution, and not be hasty to fill it unthinkingly with gods which could only be idols, bogus alternatives:

> What is this invocation? Not a hailing of those familiar to it, and not an invocation to highlight the invoker. Instead it is that invocation through which we stand in waiting for the invoked as such, and by which we first posit that which is awaited as still far removed in the distance, thus at the same time renouncing its proximity. This invocation is the taking up of a conflict between the open welcome of readiness and the absence of fulfillment. To endure such a conflict is *pain*, *suffering*, and so the invocation is a *plaint* (verse 3 ff):

> but if,
> You waters of my homeland, now with you
> The love of my heart laments. . . .

(GA 39: 81)

We have only followed Heidegger on Hölderlin through the first few lines of 'Germania' yet several crucial features of the elucidation have already come out. First, there is the transformation in basic attitudes to language, the move out of the propositional attitude. We have seen this in the opening. If this were in the conventional language of statements, then Hölderlin would merely be declaring the classical gods to be non-existent. In fact, it is an action whose effect is to open and hold open a space – that of the absence of gods – in which the poem will unfold. As Heidegger writes in 'The Letter on "Humanism"' that 'If the human being is to find his way once again into the nearness of being, he must first learn to exist in the nameless.'

Second, this brings us to one of Heidegger's crucial terms. The invocation sounds what Heidegger terms the 'fundamental tone' or 'attunement' of the poem, setting forth the emotional and intellectual world in which the poem as a whole will unfold and resonate. *Grundstimmung* ('fundamental/ground tone') is a quasi-technical term in Heidegger's elucidations of the poetic, explicitly at work in the earlier readings, implicitly in others. We must stop with it briefly.

GRUNDSTIMMUNG/'FUNDAMENTAL TONE'

Holism is once more the crucial issue. Provisionally, the *Grundstimmung* can be related to the fact, attested by many poets, that in the emergence of the poem, a sense of the whole precedes and determines the individual parts. Paul Valéry's notion of '*la ligne donnée*' is relevant here – the seeming gift to the poet of a line from nowhere, one already forceful and complete, its tone setting up a resonance in which the rest of the work is latent. To refer to just one example from the many possible, Rilke's *Duino Elegies* first came to the poet as a line seemingly dictated from out of the blue, interrupting a seemingly unrelated train of thought.

> it was as though a voice in the storm had cried out to him: '*Wer, wenn ich schriee, hörte mich denn aus der Engel Ordnungen?*' ['Who, if I cried out, among the hierarchy of angels would hear me?']. He stood still listening, 'What is it', he whispered. 'What is it that is coming?'
>
> He took out his notebook, which he always carried on him, and wrote down these words, and immediately afterward some verses formed themselves without his help.
>
> (Quoted in Fehrmann 1980: 145)

Such inspiration Rilke ascribes, traditionally, to 'the God.' Other poets attest the gift not of a specific line as such but a general sense of a possible work, emergent and insistent. Heidegger's notion of the *Grundstimmung* helps us read these episodes of 'inspiration' without the evasions of a religious terminology or the reductions of a merely psychological account. The *Grundstimmung* is the unifying fundamental source from whose impetus the poem emerges as from a nascent Gestalt. It is not primarily a state of mind within the poet, but a sense of things as newly revealed under the colouring of the emergent poem:

> the poet speaks by virtue of a tone [*Stimmung*] which sets [*bestimmt*] the ground and base and stakes out [*durchstimmt*] the space from and in which the poetic saying establishes a mode of being. This tone we name the fundamental tone of the poetry. By fundamental tone, however, we do not mean an undulating state of emotion merely accompanying the language: rather, the fundamental tone opens the world which receives the imprint of its being in poetic speech.
>
> (GA 39: 79)

A later essay on the early twentieth-century poet Georg Trakl speaks of each great poet writing out of one 'site', that of one 'poetic statement' which need never be explicit anywhere but which pervades each poem in the oeuvre. 'The site gathers unto itself, supremely, and in the extreme. Its gathering power penetrates and pervades everything' ('Language in the Poem' (1952), WL: 159). Its pull forms the 'movement-giving wave' of the poem's unfolding. It is simultaneously that *from* out of which the poem arises and *to* which each of its words is drawn. It is 'what, from a metaphysical-aesthetic point of view, may at first appear to be rhythm' (WL: 160).

What emerges as the fundamental tone of Hölderlin's 'Germania'? It is 'the oppression which holds itself in readiness in sacred mourning' – a summary statement, in effect, of the tone of the opening. This phrase becomes almost a refrain in Heidegger's reading. The distinction of Hölderlin for Heidegger is the penetration of the *Grundstimmung* of his poetry of poetry, its making explicit of the disenchantment of European humanity. Other poets may disclose various modes of being or elements of their world, but in Hölderlin, the disclosure is a matter of deep history: it concerns the destiny of the West.

This fundamental tone is not then something which Hölderlin makes up: it is attuned to a disenchantment which is already there, all pervasively but unthought, and it makes it resonate unignorably in language. The landscape itself, as the poem continues, appears under the colouring of this uncertain longing:

> For full of expectation lies
> The country, and as though it had lowered
> In sultry dog-days, on us a heaven today,
> You yearning rivers, casts prophetic shade.
> With promises it is fraught, and to me
> Seems threatening too . . .

The terminology of attunement and tonality helps Heidegger to talk about the emergence and working of the poetic in ways which avoid a crude language of linear cause and effect. The subtlety is this: on the one hand the poetic with its fundamental tone is not something that happens in the writer's head, as a mood or a thought and which then colours his or her representation of reality in language. The poet is essentially passive in relation to the tone. It comes *to* the poet, as in classical theories of inspiration, as an apprehension of the world under a deeper and defamiliarizing sense. In that revelation the poet responds to something that comes from the outside. On the other hand (and this seems at first a contradiction), neither is the tone something merely there already in the world and which the poet must subsequently translate into words. It resonates from out of the poet's listening to the language and it needs the act of the poet to sound out and be apprehensible. Where does this leave us then? Does the revelation come first or the words? The answer is that there is only a contradiction here on the surface, for linear thinking. The revelation of the world in the resonance of the ground tone and its coming to language for the poet are simultaneous or equi-primordial. It all takes place too holistically – too non-foundationally – to be disentangled in terms of any one element being the 'cause' and the other an 'effect' (cf. E: 80).

'Germania', the first poem Heidegger ever treated in depth, bears out a holistic principle that recurs in all his later readings of poetry. A poem such as 'Germania' resists a thematic reading, for its every word is charged with the singular force of a whole projected in the *Grundstimmung*. Every word bears a peculiar and unique inflection: the word-meanings could not be spelled out individually by resorting to a dictionary (think, for instance, of going to a dictionary to interpret Blake's words 'O rose thou art sick'). Heidegger's prose stretches itself to the limit in trying to describe, in the linear succession of normal words, the working of the poetic text as a happening all at once, backwards and forwards:

> Beyond the choice, the place or enchainment of the words, it is . . . above all the whole rhythmic configuration of the poetic word which 'expresses' what one calls the meaning. This rhythmic assemblage of saying is not, however, primarily the result of the placement of the words and the disposition of the verse, but in fact the other way round: the rhythmic configuration is first, the creative vibrancy first intuiting the language, the constant and all-pervading source, pre-resonant with the ranging of words, and it presides not only over the distribution and the placement of words but also their selection. The rhythmic configuration of the speaking is yet determined from the outset by the fundamental tone of the poem which obtains its form in the inner contours of the totality.
>
> (GA 39: 14–15)

For Heidegger the primary task of the reader in preserving a poem is to become attuned, non-conceptually, to the fundamental tone: 'At the heart of the sphere of power of the poetry, we should first determine the place from which and towards which the power of the poetry opens itself and remains powerful' (GA 39: 139). This is simultaneously a transformation of our attitude to language and a putting into question of ourselves, the readers, as users of language. We should no longer be thinking of the poem as something we can know as being 'about' something, but as opening a space of its own projection for us to inhabit, possessing us like a dance or a walk to music. 'Giving the tonality, [the poetry] should attune us to the place from which the totality of being opens itself to a new experience' (GA 39: 137).

We enter the poem as a 'rhythmic' space attuning us anew, one in which we must give up the sense that we are already sure what its terms (such as 'the gods') mean and who we are who so represent them to ourselves. In short, we must conceive ourselves as addressees of and participators in the poem, and no longer as its historians or its aesthetic connoisseurs. A section of Heidegger's lecture on 'Germania' directly turns to the audience as a sample of the German people, and works to unsettle all their complacencies about who they are, where they are in history and even what that history, at bottom, really is.

POETIC IMAGES

Having worked through 'Germania' this far, the rest of the poem may seem to fall into place fairly easily. Hölderlin turns to figurative language for the rest of the ode, which is a kind of prophecy. Three images in particular stand out, the figure of a man, perhaps the poet, who is looking expectantly to the east, and also the images of an eagle and of the girl called Germania.

In the third strophe the depiction of a land in expectation centres on the figure of the solitary man looking to the Orient. It is this figure who sees the approach of an eagle coming originally from the Indus, a messenger from 'the gods' it seems. The rest of the poem is this messenger's address to 'Germania,' a girl virginal and self-effacing in accordance with Hölderlin's irenic patriotism.

Yet, the eagle's annunciation is also obscure. What is Germania being exhorted to do or say?

O drink the morning breezes
Until you are opened up
And name what you see before you;
No longer now the unspoken
May remain a mystery
Though long it has been veiled . . .

It seems here that she is to become a kind of super-Hölderlinian poet, one whose speech transforms the very sight of what it names, according to Hölderlin's ideal of art. This might seem relatively accessible in the context of Hölderlin's hopes for a new beginning for his people. It is an annunciation, that 'A truth be made a manifest', surely that of the possibility of a new destiny. Yet the strophe also ends exhorting that what Germania might say be 'Yet unuttered also, just as it was found, / So let it, innocent virgin, remain'! David Constantine writes that the eagle's message is 'a strangely contorted and obscure celebration of Germania's qualities, and his instructions are manifestly impossible to obey' (Constantine 1988: 257). So in the end we seem 'no further forward' (ibid). The annunciation is premature: it seems to withdraw itself in its very gift! The overall movement of the ode remains that of a hope without an object, just as, at the close of 'Homecoming' the poet, with his mission, remained alone.

How does Heidegger deal with this section, the bulk in fact of the poem? His argument so far might suggest that the scene of the eagle and Germania relates to the fundamental tone, especially its doubleness of both loss and expectation. Now, we might think, in this annunciation the more forward-looking, prophetic aspect of the fundamental tone will come to the fore.

This seems reasonable, but Heidegger's reading is not of this sort. For Heidegger, Hölderlin's turning to images cannot be read so easily. Instead, there is a return to general considerations.

Our temptation is to put into practice the assumption that poetic images must be read by our translating their obscurity into something already familiar – we reason that since it obviously cannot be a matter of a real eagle talking to a young German girl, the images must express a prophetic expectancy for a new beginning in Germany, and so on perhaps, in the kind of crossword-puzzle solving which exercises on poetry too often become. Yet this seemingly common-sense way of proceeding is exactly what Heidegger contests. To read thus is not to do justice to the *Grundstimmung*, to the holistic kind of reading it requires or the kind of transformation of basic attitudes in ourselves which that demands. The point is that by decoding these images in a traditional way – restating the initially obscure in terms of the already known – we will have reduced the *Grundstimmung* to a mere theme or idea represented by language (see also GA 75: 69–70). We have ignored Heidegger's injunction to read and become attuned to the poetry itself poetically and have rather subordinated poetry to representationalist thinking, slipping back into the knowing attitude – probably quite innocently, so all-pervasive are the modes of thought and being we need to put at stake.

What does Heidegger give us then? The images, he argues, must offer themselves to our interpretation and thematization (we cannot not interpret after all!), but we must also preserve the singularity and strangeness of what is said, undecoded, unthematized and resistant to our totalizing efforts. The text must be recognized as holding back, as well as offering forth. This is the matter of the singularity of the work once more. In the 'Origin of the Work of Art', given as a lecture not many months later, it is what will concern Heidegger in terms of a work's 'setting forth of the earth'. The earthly, irreducible nature of the figurative language must be preserved in the kind of attention we bring to the images of the eagle and the young girl. These cannot be finalized by us as closed or settled themes or ideas, 'what Hölderlin really said' or whatever. (The crucial thing about Heidegger, as was stressed at the opening of this study, is his challenge to what 'understanding' or 'knowing' usually mean.)

Poetic language, as the bringing to word and to issue of its own primordial disclosive power, always risks falling back into more traditional kinds of language: 'language must constantly place itself into the illusion which it itself has generated, and thereby endanger what is most its own, authentic saying' (E: 55; trans. modified). Heidegger's reading of the second half of Hölderlin's 'Germania' concerns how this authenticity can be preserved against the reader's understandable if misguided reaching for familiar guiderails to steady against the disorientation of a 'poetry of poetry'. For Heidegger, the only authentic path is not to flee the disorientation to which poetic language subjects us and our seeming certainties, but to resolve to remain in it, transformed.

The reader must both thematize *and* hold open (GA 39: 121). The poetic, like the oracular (GA 39: 127), is language which manifests itself partly *as a secret*, namely, as that which legibly makes known that something is hidden, withdrawn, unsaid, without directly revealing anything but the reserve of secrecy. Such language corresponds to Hölderlin's idea of the 'sacred': if the reader lets it be and preserves its non-objectifiable, non-thematizable nature, it may, instead of becoming our object, change us. So a concern for the *Grundstimmung* is lost as soon we start conceiving it as merely what the poetry is 'about'. In fact it could never be approached in that way, for it is not any sort of object we could hold in front of us (see Ist: 119). It is the essential 'unsaid' magnetizing all that is said in a movement of disclosure as concealment (or vice versa).

From the need to preserve in the poem the demands of this kind of non-knowing knowledge, so to speak, follow all the seeming contradictions that render Heidegger on the poetic so frustrating a topic to an overly analytic philosopher – for Heidegger affirms the value of the text in an act of clarification that not only repudiates traditional methods of interpretation or contextualization, but which finally affirms that text's withdrawal from understanding. It brings the poem nearer by stressing its remoteness, so that the elucidation is a contradictory double movement of approaching and holding off, as in 'Homecoming': 'How can we preserve it – this mystery of nearness – without our knowing it? For the sake of this knowledge there must always be one who first returns home and says the mystery again and again' (E 43).

In sum, Heidegger's ideal in approaching the poetic is of a nonobjectifying non-totalizing reading in which the reader undergoes a critical defamiliarization of the very obviousness of language and the world, resonant with the transformative tone of Hölderlin's religion without an object. It is a matter not of getting at some hidden meaning but of both 'letting the unsayable be not said' and of 'doing so in and through its own speech act' (GA 39: 119) (a particularly good example of Heidegger's delight in poetry's defiance of propositional logic):

> The secret is not a barrier placed beyond the truth, but in fact truth's highest form [*Gestalt*]; for to let the secret remain truly what it is – the preservation of authentic being in its withdrawal – the secret must be manifest as such. A secret which is not apprehended in its power of veiling is not a secret.
>
> (GA 39: 119)

Heidegger's readings all affirm 'mystery', but not in any vaguely religiose sense. The quotation just given, in effect, summarizes the ideal of non-appropriative knowledge we have already seen in relation to Heidegger's reading of 'Homecoming'. There he writes that 'we never know a mystery by unveiling or analyzing it to death, but only in such a way that we preserve the mystery *as* mystery' (E 43).

Thus the matter of the poem cannot be evaded by being considered merely an attitude or idea held by Hölderlin. Both 'Homeland' and 'Germania' remain the opening of a space toward a transformed, non-objectifying mode of being. It is this that Hölderlin means by the 'homeland' (*Vaterland*), a term that Heidegger in 1934 dissociates from 'dubious and noisy' kinds of nationalism (GA 39: 120).

As the reader becomes attuned to the poem's double-edged fundamental tone, and is drawn on by a figurative prophetic language which withdraws from interpretation even as it offers itself, 'Germania' becomes the experience of a radical defamiliarization of language, identity and knowledge. It is a call to leave the complacent oblivion of our current certainties and endure the 'pain' of an authentic sense of the uncanny, unhomely 'homeland'.

Heidegger's readings of Hölderlin take the reader up to the very limit of traditional presuppositions. At times, perhaps, Heidegger does not resist the temptation to go farther and to flesh out, using Hölderlin, some would-be post-metaphysical mythology, and he has been criticized for this (see next chapter). In the reading of 'Germania,' however, the 'homeland' is anything but a place of assurance. It is a site of felt lack, endurance and of an expectation that cannot know its own measure, one drawing all the received terms of poetics – form, image, content – into a 'whirlpool' (GA 39: 136).

SUMMARY

After his controversial and abortive engagement with politics in the early days of Germany's Nazi government, Heidegger turned to art and the poetic, above all to the German romantic poet Friedrich Hölderlin. Heidegger was attentive in the poetic to the possibility that here might be a space outside of the dominance of productionist thinking. Heidegger uses the German term *Dichtung* to name the genuinely poetic, with all the characteristics of a true work of art as described in 'The Origin of the Work of

Art'. He reserved the term 'literature' to the usual object of literary criticism, i.e. work merely determined by the cultural debates of its day.

Heidegger's readings of *Dichtung* aim for a drastic transformation in the deepest assumptions of the reader. He rejects the ways in which the poetic is recuperated by critical and educational institutions. These, in effect, reduce it to something safely compatible with dominant thinking and the oppressive world of globalized techno-science (this is whether the approach is to see the work merely in terms of some extractable content, or an historical document merely to be situated in its more immediate cultural context, or as an object of formal analysis, attentive to its generic and rhetorical structures). For Heidegger, the only context that matters is deep history. For him, Hölderlin's work stands out for its untimely engagement with European nihilism (the death of the gods in Hölderlin's parlance). This makes this early nineteenth-century poet absolutely contemporary, and indeed ahead of us, in his practice.

Out of his symbiotic relationship with Hölderlin's thought and practice Heidegger's reading strives towards the ideal of a non-appropriative understanding of the poetic. This is sensitive to the way Hölderlin's *Dichtung* draws the patient reader into a revelation of its (and our) world as one of nihilism, of the absence of the sacred. So negative a revelation however, is also the first stage in the making room for a new sense of the sacred in Hölderlin's sense. The sacred is at work already in the poetic act as a kind of paradoxical knowing other than that of metaphysical thinking. This is an non-exploitative mode of knowledge that addresses but does not negate the otherness of what it touches. It lets 'the unsayable be not said', and makes truly clear by leaving a reserve of mystery.

7

NAZISM, POETRY AND THE POLITICAL

Heidegger and Nazism: the issues are so contentious, so overdeter-
mined by contemporary intellectual politics, and some of the concerns
so horrific that this is a topic about which it is probably impossible to
think straight. The controversy was stirred to new life by a book
by Victor Farias (1989). Farias's argument that Heidegger was a Nazi
throughout his life and his work thoroughly fascist is easy to dismiss.
Less dismissable is evidence gleaned by other scholars at this time,
notably Hugo Ott (1993), revealing the extent and depth of Heidegger's involvement with the Nazis in the 1930s. This refutes some of
Heidegger's own defensive self-presentations on these issues.

Farias's book said little new. At times, this was an opportunistic
book, engineering a *succès de scandale* by making extreme claims bound
to grab the attention of a lot of people. It owed its impact to the way
the figure it attacked had become, by the mid-1980s, an indispensable
reference in radical modern thinking, especially in continental Europe,
where Heidegger's thinking had become newly prominent with the
decline of Marxism. This association gave the debate its seeming stakes
and its peculiar vehemence. The oddity remains that it is often more
conservative thinkers who are eager to dismiss Heidegger, while those
who defend the continuing value of his thought are broadly of the left.

What is incontestable is that Heidegger joined the Nazi party in May
1933 and that during 1933–4 at least his political engagement was a

matter of genuine conviction and even excitement. In May 1933 Heidegger was elected by his colleagues to serve as Rector of Freiburg University. Heidegger later claimed that he accepted this post reluctantly with a view to helping protect the University from the new regime that had come to power earlier that year. In fact, he took a leading role in the 'bringing into line' (*Gleichschaltung*) of German university life, producing several speeches and newspaper articles in support of the regime and even calling himself the 'Führer' of the University. The extent to which Heidegger was anti-Semitic is open to debate. His writings from the 1920s and 1930s stand out – such was the context – for the absence of racism, which Heidegger explicitly attacked in lectures. Nevertheless, in academic politics Heidegger was prepared to appeal to the anti-Semitism of others if it helped get his own way. A letter proving this was among evidence cited in Heidegger's case before the Denazification Committee of the French occupying force in 1946. Overall, Heidegger was convicted for having 'in the crucial year of 1933 . . . consciously placed the great prestige of his scholarly reputation and the distinctive art of his oratory in the service of the National Socialist Revolution . . . thereby doing a great deal to justify this revolution in the eyes of educated Germans' (Ott 1993: 327). The committee suspended Heidegger from teaching, a ban lifted in 1950.

How far Heidegger continued his support for National Socialism after 1933 is one of the issues of contention. He certainly remained a member of the party till 1945, though of course, in a totalitarian state, resignation would not have been prudent. Heidegger dated his disillusion with the Nazis from the so-called 'Night of the Long Knives', 30 June 1934, when the particular party faction he felt closest to was purged (Rec: 499). He then seems to have reached an ambivalent position, defending some increasingly idiosyncratic lost 'essence' of National Socialism against what it was in reality. The lectures on the origin of the work of art and the first lectures on Hölderlin both emerge from this especially imponderable time. A lecture course of 1935 attacked 'works being peddled about nowadays as the philosophy of National Socialism' compared to what Heidegger clung to as the lost 'inner truth and greatness' of the movement, a statement reprinted in 1953 (IM: 213). In the late 1930s, Heidegger's lectures on Friedrich Nietzsche (N) make up a clear if coded attack on Nazism as a merely another, late nihilistic form of productionist metaphysics.

For the rest of his life Heidegger's view of Hitler's coming to power in early 1933 remained that the chance of a genuine national renewal had been there, one that could have led Europe away from the path of nihilism and self-destruction, but that the movement swiftly betrayed this promise. Looking back on this supposed betrayal, Heidegger blamed his fellow German intellectuals for not having tried in sufficient numbers to direct and shape events as he had tried, for allowing a racist and militarist cult to turn Nazism into merely another version of European nihilism, on a par with Stalinism or American capitalism. So Heidegger's personal version of National Socialism was very much a thing on its own, part of his tendency to self-mythologization as the prophetic thinker who may be able to lead Europe out of the shadows of a nihilistic modernity into a new dispensation of being.

We cannot consider here the debate as to whether or not Heidegger's greatest work *Being and Time* (1927) anticipates the fascist politics of 1933. *Being and Time* precedes by seven years the turn to art and the poetic in Heidegger that is our concern and which was in part a reaction to what he called the 'stupidity' of the Rectorship (Pet: 37). However, one can see how fascism is at least a possibility latent in aspects of Heidegger's thinking, if not inevitably or necessarily inscribed there. Let us return briefly to the issue of 'holism' from Chapter 1. Might not a holism which is critical and anti-reductive in its response to the dominations of scientism, bureaucratic rationalization and control – the implications taken up by so-called left-Heideggerians – become oppressive and inherently totalitarian when transferred too hastily into an active programme of immediate political change, i.e. the demand to think a state or nation *as a whole*, as more than and transcending the sum of its parts? From that perspective the people (*das Volk*) is more than the sum of its individuals. It is that whence they arise and take their identity, a position that might lead to a view of the individual's irrelevance. In the early 1930s attempts to criticize and alleviate the atomistic individualism of modern life, its solitude and alienation, led Heidegger too quickly into a dismissal of the importance of individual political and economic rights. Liberty in the modern sense of individual autonomy appears mainly as a threat to social cohesion and a would-be deeper sense of belonging to a people and place. Only, it seemed, surrender to a greater power, embodied in a leader, could ensure the genuine and nonalienating self-realization of that people in a communal movement, liberating the German worker from the yoke of capitalism and bringing in the intellectual worker in common cause. So we can surmise that a holism at work in Heidegger's critiques of theoreticism might also lead, if transferred too hastily to politics, to disturbing claims such as that made by Rector Heidegger in 1934 that 'The individual by himself counts for nothing. It is the destiny of our nation incarnated by its state that matters' (Freiburg University Archives; quoted in Ott 1993: 240).

HEIDEGGER'S SILENCE?

For many, however, the outstanding controversy about Heidegger is not his period of engagement with Nazism. It is that after the war, when the full horror of what had taken place in Germany was known, he seems to have failed fully to acknowledge it. His personal apologetics, evasive or otherwise, seem insignificant compared to this failure of thought, especially the seeming inability to confront the holocaust and think through its implications. The nature of Heidegger's silence on the holocaust is open to interpretation. Not speaking is an even stronger source of wildly competing interpretations than are Heidegger's dense writings! Unfortunately for would-be defenders of Heidegger the rare occasions when he broke that silence are morally problematic. Most famous is a seemingly off the cuff remark made in a lecture in Bremen in 1949, a remark omitted when the text reappeared as 'The Question Concerning Technology' (QCT: 1–35):

> Agriculture is now a mechanized food industry, in essence the same as the manufacture of corpses in the gas chambers and extermination camps, the same as the blockading and starving of nations, the same as the manufacture of hydrogen bombs.
>
> (Quoted in Schirmacher 1983: 25)

The sentence has outraged many for its insensitive equation of food production and mass murder (see Milchman and Rosenberg 1996). Heidegger's primary topic is not the extermination itself but modern agriculture. To express his horror at the reduction of a way of life to a mere industry he seems to have reached for the most extreme instance he could conceive of the evils of technology. To say that modern farming, the holocaust and the hydrogen bomb have 'the same essence' means that they all manifest a world in which technology structures fundamentally the way things appear. This may well be true, but can it justify the kind of blanket equivalence in Heidegger's sentence? It has been argued that Heidegger's standpoint, of always homing in on what is said on the largest scale, of being and of history only in the sense of changes in what is historically decisive, *geschichtlich*, blinds him to history in its more familiar sense. However, even this statement about agriculture and the holocaust has been defended. For some, Heidegger's equation is primarily a warning about the future, the coming technological devastation of the earth and of humanity (Young 1997: 181–5). Likewise it is not impossible to present Heidegger's post-war philosophy as in part a response to the holocaust. His work is after all a meditation on the nihilistic essence of the modern West, revealing its threat not only to life but to the human essence itself conceived in terms of the openness to being. From this respect, there might even seem something appropriate in Heidegger's public silence on the murder of the European Jews, when set against a society dominated by what he termed 'publicity' and the media, whose crass representations increasingly determine what is generally taken as real. Why reduce this unspeakable event to the level of representations that glibly circulate as 'news events'? Heidegger wrote to the Jewish poet Paul Celan on 30 January 1968, after their meeting in July that 'Since then we have much to have been silent about together' ('*Seitdem haben wir vieles einander zugeschwiegen*') (quoted in Emmerich 1999: 144–5).

The view of Heidegger's silence as appropriate may seem generous. Nevertheless, discussions of this issue from post-Heideggerian philosophers draw deeply on Heidegger's thinking in approaching the holocaust, even while repudiating what seem Heidegger's own failings. In Philippe Lacoue-Labarthe's work, what might be termed a Heideggerian reading of the holocaust is suggested, supplementing that which Heidegger's published work seems merely to hint. Lacoue-Labarthe takes up the concept of *Geschichte*, the history of being conceived as a series of shifts in the most fundamental sense of human things. For Lacoue-Labarthe, unlike Heidegger, the holocaust *is* such a decisive shift, and not just one event among others manifesting the nihilism of the modern world. It is a deep historical break (*geschichtlich*) in the sense that nothing afterwards can be the same. For Lacoue-Labarthe, drawing on Heidegger's reading of nihilism, 'Auschwitz' is a horrific revelation of the nature of Western civilization, and it 'opens up, or closes, a quite other history than the one we have known up until now' (Lacoue-Labarthe 1990: 45).

Perhaps, though, Heidegger was right: 'We may find Heidegger barbarically insensitive in his refusal to speak to the Shoah in his *Seins-geschichte* [history of being], but our horror does not 'negate' his or any view that does not find in the holocaust a radical rupture in the possibilities open to Western thought' (Lysaker 1993: 206). Does world history since 1945 perhaps support Heidegger's seemingly brutal remark that the Second World War essentially decided nothing (WT: 66)? Among those who agree with this disturbing view is the French philosopher Jean-François Lyotard who elaborates what is recognizably a variant Heideggerian reading of the extermination (Lyotard 1990). Lyotard endorses the argument that the holocaust manifests the violence inherent in Western rationality, without, like Lacoue-Labarthe, seeing this horrific revelation as marking a deep historical (*geschichtlich*) break. Nevertheless Heidegger, in Lyotard's view, still remains convicted of a disastrous inability to make moral distinctions. There are two broad aspects of Heidegger's blindness. First, to see the holocaust as a mani-festation of European nihilism in general is to evade the specific German responsibility for the murders. Second, Lyotard argues that Heidegger cannot even pose, let alone answer the question, 'why mainly the Jews?'

Lyotard's, Blanchot's (Blanchot 1993: 129ff) and George Steiner's efforts (Steiner 1992: 45) to find some rationale as to why the Jews in particular were victimized offer again a kind of revisionist Heideg-gerianism. Each sees the issue in relation to the repressed insecurities of Western modernity, in its drive to provide a self-sufficient rationale for human life based solely on a secular viewpoint. Against this drive, they argue, the Jews offered the discomforting challenge of a people who insist on the finitude of human life and knowledge and who main-tain the necessity of some sort of relation to the divine. They pose a challenge in their very existence to the secular principles of moder-nity. But is this argument convincing? Is it not to attribute to anti-Semitism a greater knowledge of Judaism than is plausible, giving it even something of the dignity of an intellectual position?

ART AND POLITICS

How do these issues relate to Heidegger's thinking about art and the poetic? The writings on the poetic all postdate his Rectorship and are generally read as a reaction against it. The years 1934–6 show an increasingly critical attitude towards any notion of politics itself still centred on the human will alone and on competing world-views. Heidegger's unscheduled decision to lecture on Hölderlin in 1934–5 was a turn to a kind of quietist 'spiritual' politics geared towards fundamental attunements and receptivity to being, incompatible with active programmes of social planning or merely institutional change.

This introduction has necessarily already implied a position on this issue, effectively arguing that, from the time of the engagement with Hölderlin in late 1934, Heidegger eschewed direct political action in his hopes for German renewal and re-engaged in a deeper critique of the bases of Western history in productionist metaphysics, a critique whose main impact must be a grim realization of the extent to which its totalitarian anthropocentrism touches every aspect of modern life and thought.

One of the most influential books on this topic is again Philippe Lacoue-Labarthe's *Heidegger, Art and Politics*, published in 1987, just before Farias's assault. Lacoue-Labarthe shows that it is not possible to talk about 'Heidegger and politics' as if the term politics was without a set of assumptions about which Heidegger has a lot to say. Politics in the traditional sense, argues Lacoue-Labarthe, has been a function of productionist thinking: it has always been conceived in the West as a form of technics or craft, namely that of the fashioning or making of a people according to some idea or ideal of their life together (as a potter moulds a pot towards the shape of its preconceived design). Nazism was striking for the way it intensified this association of politics and a kind of craft, for it stressed the genuine essence of Germany as something the German people should continuously create in their daily life and activities, all of which in turn become celebrated as the expression of a common essence and destiny. It is an essence made visible in flags, insignia, uniforms and in such large scale productions as the infamous Nuremberg rally or the propagandist films of Leni Riefenstahl, as well as in the ruthless elimination of everything and everyone considered non-German. Against this, Lacoue-Labarthe argues, Heidegger offered his own revisionist reading of the relation of art and politics. So, what might 'politics' mean for Heidegger? Again, Heidegger's thinking moves by taking the terms of Western life back to their Greek source, so opening the space for a new beginning at the same, profound level. In 1935, Heidegger lectures that 'state' or 'city', or 'city-state' are inadequate terms to translate the Greek '*polis*'. '*Polis*' 'means rather, the historical [*geschichtlich*] place, the there *in* which and *out* of which, and *for* which history happens' (IM: 162–3). So any making or production of a people in the conventional understanding of politics must presuppose and take place within some given 'world', that basic structuring of human existence which is 'political' in a deeper sense. In other words, the only 'politics' that can truly matter for Heidegger, or makes for any essential kind of change, is deep history, *Geschichte*.

Heidegger believed till the end of his life that although it had been quickly perverted, there had been the possibly of a genuinely 'deep historical' or *geschichtlich* change in Germany in the early 1930s, i.e. a shift in the most basic attitudes and 'world'. The 'Origin of the Work of Art' (lectured in 1936), still includes the 'founding' of a state as a possible new instituting of truth alongside thinking and art, though this disappears altogether in lectures later in the 1930s. The work on art and on Hölderlin is then a more fundamental continuation of the drive to renewal that had taken a more conventional 'political' form in 1933. In his apologia, 'The Rectorate 1933/4: Facts and Thoughts,' Heidegger writes:

> What is essential is that we are caught in the consummation of nihilism, that God is 'dead', and every time-space for the godhead covered up. The surmounting of nihilism nevertheless announces itself in German poetic thinking and singing. Of this poetry, however, the Germans still have had the least understanding, because they are concerned to adapt to the measures of the nihilism that surrounds them.

(Rec: 498)

In Heidegger's understanding, this issue alone is genuinely 'political' in the sense of a historically decisive change in the worlding of the world. His reference to 'what is German', for all its latent nationalism, is very distant from the racist and exclusive Nazi essentialism. It seeks, in the German language and people, the possibility of a new non-reductive relation to being, one which would both repeat and revise the Greek inauguration of Western life.

So is the excruciating difficulty of thinking through Heidegger's politics thankfully eased for the reader whose main interest is in literature? Not entirely. This alternative, essential 'politics' centred on Hölderlin and art, still makes some people uncomfortable, and not only for its German-centric stance. For Lacoue-Labarthe the problem has less to do with Heidegger's destructive/deconstructive readings of traditional notions of interpretation, meaning, history etc. but with what might be termed the more recuperative side of his elucidations. Heidegger is too eager to reach some 'other thinking', outside the closure of productionist metaphysics. As a result his readings of poetry are sometimes an idealization. Heidegger is premature. Lacoue-Labarthe suggests that the 'Hölderlinian preaching', as he calls it (Lacoue-Labarthe 1990: 12), is too often tempted into a dogmatic mythologizing. Lacoue-Labarthe's reservations concern the mythological motifs derived from Hölderlin in Heidegger's later thinking, the 'fourfold,' the lack of sacred names, the call for new gods, etc.. These contrast with the tortured but more scrupulously defensible recognition of other Heidegger texts (e.g. 'On the Question of Being,' P: 291–322) that one cannot so directly exit the language and thinking of the tradition, that its hold on us is too total to admit yet of more than a patient tracing of its all pervading closure.

Lacoue-Labarthe's argument has been very influential. Heidegger has been charged with allegorizing some of the texts he reads in the light of his own hopes for a step out of metaphysical nihilism, contrary to the more chastened, perhaps despairing elements in the poetry itself. He tends not to see the time of pain of Hölderlin, Trakl and others but in terms of the coming of a new wholeness, or to see loss except as potentially the space for a new advent. Véronique Fóti writes that, whether it is a question of Hölderlin's poetry, Hölderlin's speculations on Greek tragedy just before the onset of his madness, or Trakl's poetry from the First World War, Heidegger is unable, strangely, to countenance loss and disaster fully, as such, outside the redemptive possibility of some hidden saving power (Fóti 1992: 74). John D. Caputo likewise argues that Heidegger holds 'poetry's most disturbing and menacing effects in check' (Caputo 1993: 148). Hölderlin's tentative and unsettled thinking on the possibility of new gods becomes sometimes too definite a programme in Heidegger's Hölderlin.

One issue is that the central concept of the 'history of being' provides just too monolithic a frame in which to deal with the singularity of the poetic or with much that is usually recognized of importance in literature. John Caputo writes of Heidegger's essay on Georg Trakl that whereas poetry has always been celebrated as one place where the cry of individual pain can sound out, from Heidegger's deep historical perspective the empirical pain of any one person would be a 'merely anthropological' concern (Caputo 1993: 149). Heidegger's remorseless attention to essential and historical (*geschichtlich*) issues makes his work profound, but it also renders it oddly etherializing or, precisely, essentializing. This point has already come up in relation to the infamous agriculture remark. Factical pain, in itself, is downplayed except as Heidegger can read Trakl's poetry in terms of its historically disclosive or concealing power, i.e. as a mode of unconcealment or concealment in the history of being. Pain, or emotions such as love, anger, compassion etc., not having the status of rising to fundamental attunements, are simply not in the game of either disclosing or concealing anything and so fall to the side of the thinker's path as inessential. These would be very much the limitations of a specifically philosophical reading. Despite the arguments of 'The Origin of the Work of Art', the poetic is not given its full singularity, but is still being weighed predominantly as a means of knowledge, albeit in a radically altered form. In the reading of Hölderlin's 'Andenken' even love is considered as essentially a mode of truth (E: 147–8).

The argument then, elaborated at length in Fóti's influential *Heidegger and the Poets* (1992), is that Heidegger's concern with the 'history of being' and the possibility of a major transformation in Western history becomes a restrictive personal mythology, a 'grand narrative' that imposes itself upon the texts Heidegger reads. First, the themes of the oblivion of being and of awakening a fundamental attunement of mourning become unifying concerns that can override such normal details of scholarship as the status of the editions of the texts used, or other elements resistant to the overall focus on 'essential' questions. Heidegger relies on two editions of Hölderlin's poems, using at first the classic edition of Norbert von Hellingrath, and later the newly edited Stuttgart edition initiated in 1943. In some cases, the minutiae of Heidegger's interpretation bear upon a version of the text that is disputable, surely a major issue for readings that rest so closely on unravelling crucial words in the text (Fóti 1992: 44ff; Derrida 1995: 316).

Fóti's accusation that Heidegger cannot conceive radical loss in his readings of Hölderlin and Trakl concerns more than the accuracy of the interpretations. It relates to the greater issue of the adequacy or otherwise of Heideggerian thinking to face contemporary reality. Heidegger's alleged failure to measure up to the historically decisive character of the holocaust marks Fóti's reading, and gives it a certain tendentiousness. She is taking up a position, first articulated by the

Marxist Theodor Adorno (1903–69), that after the holocaust the very possibility of poetry must be in doubt (Fóti 1992: 74). This is why two chapters, a whole third of this short book, are devoted to the poetry of Paul Celan, a poet whom Heidegger admired as the greatest living poet, standing 'further forward than anyone else', but did not actually write about (Safranski 1998: 422). Celan was a Jewish German-speaking writer who produced some of the greatest post-war poetry in Europe. He was well read in Heidegger's thinking, as the poems show, but also, given Heidegger's past, deeply uncertain about him. Fóti, Lacoue-Labarthe and others read Celan's poetry as articulating a post-Heideggerian ethic and poetic, one that gives full witness to disaster, irrecuperable loss and the possible impossibility of poetry after the holocaust. No wonder then that a first meeting between Heidegger and Celan in 1967 has attained the status of a mythic touchstone in discussion of Heidegger and poetic (see, for instance, Lacoue-Labarthe 1999: 33–8; Golb 1988; Rapaport 1997:118–32). Heidegger and Celan were to meet twice subsequently, before Celan's suicide in 1970. Interpretations of the poem that Celan wrote after the first meeting are as at odds with each other as everything else in this tortured debate. Entitled 'Todtnauberg', the poem is named for the place of the meeting at Heidegger's country cabin (Celan 1983: II, 255). The two men had set out on a walk together after Celan had written in Heidegger's guest book: 'Into the cabin logbook, with a view towards the Brumenstern, with hope of a coming word in the heart' (Safranksi 1998: 423). Some, like Heidegger's biographer Safranksi and Hans Georg Gadamer read the poem as the record of a positive encounter (Gadamer 1985: 53). Safranski cites evidence that Celan was 'elated' after meeting Heidegger (Safranski 1998: 424). Others, however, see 'Todtnauberg' as a poem of disillusion, with its expression of the poet's hope of a 'coming word' from Heidegger and the following of paths that lead only into a marshy swamp. A text that admits of readings so contrary is, needless to say, enigmatic. However, the consensus is towards the bleaker reading. The poem is full of images that, elsewhere in Celan's work, relate to the holocaust (Golb 1988). For some readers Celan attains the status of the poet who managed to surpass the limitations of Heidegger's own poetic, writing, after Auschwitz, a poetry that gives full witness to its intolerable historic conditions and the possibility of irrecuperable loss. It thus reaches into what might be called the 'unthought' of Heidegger's own thinking.

In sum, Lacoue-Labarthe and Fóti pick up a totalizing tendency in Heidegger's readings, along with the slightly messianic drive that betrays the 'political' nature of the readings of Hölderlin in particular, offering as they do a quietist, patriotic programme of German renewal at odds with that of the Nazis and, later, with the Americanized state of post war Germany. Fóti's critique draws on a distinction between two sorts of reading. One, the more familiar, is bent on interpretation, elucidation and, inevitably, appropriation of its text. The other is no less scholarly but its rigour forces its acknowledgement finally of a certain 'unreadability' in the text, a structural resistance to any sort of univocal interpretation or totalization. The implication is that Heidegger's elucidations draw towards but fail to become the second form of reading, slipping too often into the first. Heidegger would thus approach but finally fall short of a fully deconstructive thinking that would affirm the singularity of its text against the totalizations of historicizing/thematizing readings, and which at the same time would affirm a limit of unreadability out of respect for that which eludes the grasp of our own thinking, for otherness. Fóti's is a version of an argument made many times since the 1960s: that Heidegger prepares the space for his most famous disciple, Jacques Derrida, but is still marked by residues of metaphysical thinking not at work in the latter. For instance, if Heidegger affirms the withdrawn secret nature of the text, as we saw in relation to the second part of 'Germania', it is insofar as such obscurity is seen in its 'earthly' sheltering aspect, as protecting the fundamental tone from misappropriation, not as a mere obscurity or indecipherability of the letter of the text and no more. Unlike in Celan, the failure of language itself does not seem to be countenanced fully as a possibility, but only in terms of the recuperative notion of the protective 'secret'. Thus even the very opacity of the text is put to work by Heidegger in the task of potential disclosure.

Yet, one can go a long way towards answering Fóti's accusations. Can Heidegger's stress on the poetic as a movement of fundamental questioning really be presented as a dogmatism? Gerald Bruns *Heidegger's Estrangements* (1989) discovers another Heidegger, one for whom the poetic is what might be termed a language of the 'earth' in the sense of that which is recalcitrant to thought, ungraspable, chastening:

poetry *exposes* thinking to language, to its strangeness or otherness, its refusal to be contained within categories and propositions, its irreducibility to sameness and identity, its resistance to sense – in short, its denial of our efforts to speak it. Philosophy by contrast is thinking that closes itself off to the experience with language, turns itself over to logic, tries to protect itself by bringing language under the control of the proposition. Poetry, of course, knows no such control; poetry is the letting-go of language.

(Bruns 1989: xxiv–xxv)

As the site of such an event in the most fundamental human environment, namely language, the poetic is to be preserved as the supreme site of openness to otherness, to a future not already predictable as the result of calculative processes. Although Heidegger's readings sometimes contain a rhetoric of 'homecoming' that threatens to close off this space, to identify Heideggerian poetics merely with a mythical–political programme of German renewal is too reductive, and amounts to a refusal to bear the insecurity of the open space to which Heidegger leads us. At worst, some readings of Heidegger in the 1990s, a decade marked by a deeply moralistic tendency in criticism, give to Nazism and the holocaust the status of a key to all mythologies in Heidegger's difficult texts. For Heidegger, it is most often a space of endurance and patience that Hölderlin's poetry opens.

Lyotard writes:

What art can do is bear witness not to the sublime, but to this aporia [undecidability] of art and to its pain. It does not say the unsayable, but says that it cannot say it. 'After Auschwitz' it is necessary, according to Eli Wiesel, to add yet another verse to the story of the forgetting of the recollection beside the fire in the forest. I cannot light the fire, I do not know the prayer, I can no longer find the spot in the forest, I cannot even tell the story any longer. All I know how to do is to say that I no longer know to tell this story. And this should be enough. This has to be enough. Celan 'after' Kafka, Joyce 'after' Proust, Nono 'after' Mahler.

(Lyotard 1990: 47)

And Heidegger's reading of Hölderlin? Lyotard's description of modern art as possible only as the 'sublime' witness to its own impossibility is already the place of the poetic for Hölderlin. One distinction between Heidegger and the modern writers listed by Lyotard is that Heidegger places the dilemma of the death of art much earlier – another reason perhaps why he might give less the holocaust less significance in this respect than do others. Might Heidegger's reading of Hölderlin's enunciation of a non-enunciation in 'Germania' be a case of Wiesel's 'I cannot even tell the story any longer. All I know how to do is to say that I no longer know to tell this story'?

THE READERS' DILEMMA

No new work on Heidegger is likely to be considered seriously unless it acknowledges the question of his Nazism. William Spanos's *Heidegger and Criticism* (1993) fully acknowledges Heidegger's complicity in political crime but expresses dismay at the crudities of Farias's book and special issue of *Critical Inquiry* (15, Winter 1989) on Heidegger and Nazism. Spanos argues that blanket condemnations and dismissals of Heidegger need to be understood as much in relation to our own time as to his. The vilification of Heidegger after the publication of Farias's book was in part a conservative backlash against the radical forms of critique that had owed so much to him, especially the work of Michel Foucault (1926–84) on the nature of power and Jacques Derrida's 'deconstruction' (see next chapter). Heidegger, in fact, became a convenient scapegoat whereby the triumphant liberal capitalism of the 'new world order,' post-1989, could consolidate its position in the media and academy, tarring forms of radical critique with the fascist brush, especially when a second scandal arose concerning the war-time journalism of the deconstructionist critic Paul de Man. Such American complacency, writes Spanos, forgets 'the mass destruction of civilian populations in Vietnam, Dresden and Hiroshima', falsely bolstering the moral authority of the West as victor of the Cold War (Spanos 1993: xiii).

The controversy is not only about Nazism and Heidegger. It is also necessarily about the nature of reading, interpretation, textual meaning, authorial responsibility and the reader's responsibility. This is why, over and above the immense questions that Nazism raises, the Heidegger controversy is not peripheral to a book aimed principally at readers concerned in some way with literary theory. Spanos still endorses Heideggerian thinking as a basis for a kind of oppositional cultural criticism. In other words, in most of Heidegger's work a specific politics is not built fixedly into Heidegger's texts but these still produce readings that allow a critique of modern industrial society which many on the left find profound. The actual history of Heidegger's reception is a forty year witness to this and is surely already a refutation of claims that Heidegger's thinking is inherently fascistic.

What everyone would like of course, is to read Heidegger's texts and to be able to put what is complicit with Nazism on one side and the rest on the other. Is this possible? Unfortunately, probably not. The difficulty is engaged in Michael E. Zimmerman's *Heidegger's Confrontation with Modernity: Technology, Politics, Art* (1990), one of the few books that people approaching Heidegger will find clear and authoritative. Zimmerman recognizes the way the issue of reading Heidegger, especially work of the 1930s, poses questions of the nature of textual meaning. Zimmerman endorses the statement by the contemporary French sociologist Pierre Bourdieu (1930–) that Heidegger's texts are 'polysemic,' of multiple meaning, adding:

> They can be read profitably without regard to their [immediate] political implications, but they can and should *also* be read in terms of those implications. His thought cannot be reduced to the level of an ideological 'reflex' of socio-political conditions, but on the other hand it cannot be regarded as wholly detached from such conditions. Heidegger argued that because creative works – including philosophical ones – have a measure of autonomy, the author's views about those works are not privileged.
>
> (Zimmerman 1990: 38)

Heidegger's importance as a thinker for some on the radical left is a dramatic confirmation of Zimmerman's last point. Yet the intractable difficulty of this issue also appears in the peculiar strategy of presentation adopted in Zimmerman's book. One half devotes itself to a lucid account of the kind of cultural politics in which Heidegger's work can be placed in the 1920s and 1930s in Germany, the decadence of the Weimar Republic, the general disaffection with modernity, the disillusion with democracy, the hopes for national renewal, the influence of the work of Ernst Jünger on the place of technology in the modern social and political economy etc. Here, Zimmerman's is a mode of writing very familiar to workers in modern literary studies. Heidegger's texts are placed in a context of historical debate that renders them – or seems to render them – masterable as part of the cultural politics of their day. The arguments about technology, about the hopes for a revival of the power of art, all seem to fall into place in the intellectual life of Germany at this time. The second part of Zimmerman's study is more strictly 'philosophical', working through Heidegger's arguments with productionist metaphysics, its history, its culmination in technology and in thinkers such as Jünger for whom humanity is the 'labouring animal,' etc. This is all extremely helpful, yet the division of Zimmerman's book into two parts simultaneously represents and evades the major problem in writing on Heidegger and cultural history: that Heidegger's own arguments are directed partly against the very kind of reading that Zimmerman's first section employs, namely the reduction of a poetic or philosophical text to being a function of social and historical debate, the supposed expression of its age and, with this view, the exaltation of the historian of such texts to a commanding overview whose objectivizing assumptions are not at stake. Zimmerman knowingly practices upon Heidegger exactly the kind of historicist reading that Heidegger refuses and tries to refute in the case of Hölderlin, Plato and others.

So, as Zimmerman would no doubt be the first to acknowledge, his contextualizing of Heidegger's lecture on Hölderlin's 'Germania' is a partial reading. To read only with a view to its most immediate context necessarily construes Heidegger's text as only a historical document with a particular cultural programme, and not, for example, as a movement of thought with truth claims we still need to confront. The lecture emerges as a topical programme of German renewal, based on Hölderlin, and in debate with the racist poetics of contemporaries of Heidegger, such as E. G. Kolbenheyer's version in 1932 of an 'expressivist' poetic according to which the poetry is a necessary 'biological' expression of a people (GA 39: 27). Zimmerman brings to life what Heidegger's listeners would have picked up in 1934–5. However, the difficulty – or importance – of reading Heidegger is that one cannot stop there, for deep assumptions about historicism and interpretation are exactly what is at stake in Heidegger and why he still engages us. If he were just the diminishing figure of historical perspective there would be no controversy. More than any other body of thought, Heidegger's is remarkable for the way it questions and rereads its context or any context in which one would wish to contain it.

Baldly speaking, Heidegger's concern is with *Geschichte*, a deep historical context we still share. Such fundamental assumptions about being change rarely and thus lie outside 'history' in its more quotidian sense, but when they do shift they change everything with them. Zimmerman, conventionally and lucidly, reads in terms of *Historie*. Such a reading makes itself vulnerable to the Heideggerian charge that its historicism indulges fundamental assumptions about being, objectification, historical meaning etc. that the lecture explicitly contests. Heidegger attacks that approach which 'situates itself by principle and from the first outside of the matter it judges and considers, making of it a simple object of its opinion' (GA 39: 28).

Yet does this mean we must simply side with Heidegger against Zimmerman's approach in that part of his book? It is hard to see how anyone can yet deal fully with this question. It would require engagement in philosophical issues at Heidegger's own level, with comparable acumen of thought and depth of reading in the history of philosophy. Very few are equal to this. On the other hand, the last thing anyone wants to merely to take Heidegger at his word. There is an impasse here.

Any writing on Heidegger has to think through this issue in some way or another. Zimmerman's double strategy of presentation – cultural history in part one, issues in philosophy in part two – is one way of dealing with it. It may be in tension with Heidegger's thinking, but it also responds to the impossibility of deciding where, in Heidegger's texts, one can say that such or such a concept or argument is 'fascist' or not. This is especially problematic of texts from the mid-1930s when Heidegger was developing a critical position in relation to Nazism. There is no simple test or rule that would decide for us once and for all whether elements in 'The Origin of the Work of Art' might be complicit with Nazism or not. Not only is the reading of Heidegger's texts an open-ended and often difficult process, but such readings we might undertake cannot but engage with – or assume – issues in the nature of interpretation on which Heidegger already has much to say. After all, are we even so sure we know exactly where fascism ends and other less vilifiable modes of thought begin? Jacques Derrida points out that Heidegger is far from alone at this time in diagnosing a deep and possibly terminal crisis in the idea of Europe, or in calling for a radical revolution and revaluation at the deepest level. Does such a comparable sense of extreme crisis in Edmund Husserl, Paul Valéry and other great thinkers at this time not blur the issues (Derrida 1989: 61)?

Derrida concludes that Heidegger's modern reader is placed in an impossible but also unavoidable position. We are pulled in opposite directions by two opposed demands; first, that of the need to condemn at once every mark of complicity with Nazism in Heidegger and yet, second, that of the demand for patient thought and rereading of the texts, which means of course keeping open in many circumstances

the decision as to what is complicit and what is not. There is no rule
that would decide for us:

> why isn't the case closed? why is Heidegger's trial never over and done with?
> . . . we have to, we've *already* had to, respect the possibility *and* impossibility
> of this rule: *that it remains to come.*
>
> (Derrida 1995: 193–4)

In this respect, the reading of Heidegger becomes an extreme
example of the ethical dilemma of reading more generally, in any significant text. We are torn between conclusive interpretation or judgement
and openness and re-reading. This intractable difficulty continues to be
endured in Heidegger's legacy. There is no pat 'Students' Introduction'
formula for this issue. Its strain is one reason debate about Heidegger
so easily becomes polarized, and tempers frayed. Each reader must
confront the issue anew, as his or her circumstances best allow.

AFTER HEIDEGGER

It appears to be time to think with Heidegger against Heidegger.

(Jürgen Habermas, 1953)

After Heidegger? Heidegger died in 1976, but we are not after Heidegger. His work engages questions at the most fundamental level imaginable about the nature of a human existence and what we have come to understand as knowledge. His thinking touches on about every field of intellectual work. So there is no 'after' Heidegger in the sense of something that can now be understood at a distance or put 'back into context' – for that context is what we inhabit, the globalized, industrialized and industrializing world whose basis is productionist metaphysics.

Heidegger's overall influence on modern thought is simply too vast to document in a book focused primarily on questions of the poetic. As well as transforming poetics, Heidegger is an unavoidable reference point in any discussion of the distinctive character of the West, of the nature of technology, of the nature of history and of historical study, of environmental ethics, of the nature and limits of science, of religion, of medicine and psychoanalysis, of the nature of Nazism, of the relation of the West and Asian thought, and so on. To give just one instance, Heidegger's work must have profound consequences for the idea of a university: it raises new questions about the nature and basis of an institution whose existence is already an uneasy compromise between political and social forces and intellectual work supposedly dominated by reason alone. Heidegger never withdrew the address he gave on being installed as Rector of Freiburg University in 1933, where he criticized the modern institution's lack of anything but a pragmatic basis for its foundation, and called for 'the task of retrieving from the merely technical organization of the university a new meaning which could come out of a reflection on the tradition of Western European thought' (Only: 96).

What of Heidegger's effect upon the specific field of literary study? If it is matter of influence in the sense of critics referring back frequently to Heidegger for guidance, as they have often done with Jacques Derrida, Michel Foucault, Mikhail Bakhtin and others, then apart from some books in the 1970s Heidegger is scarcely prominent. There remains no Heideggerian school of literary criticism. Gerald Bruns observes that 'for many literary critics and theorists, he is more interesting for his involvement with National Socialism than for his writings on poetry and language' (Bruns 1994: 375). However, if it is a matter of the general structures of thought from which critics draw, then Heidegger is surely a more decisive figure than any other.

Heidegger's thinking cannot be hardened as a doctrine with norms against which disciples could be ranged and judged. There can be no Heideggerian orthodoxy. A distinction one sometimes hears is that between 'left-Heideggerians' and 'right-Heideggerians'. 'Right-Heideggerians' would be those thinkers for whom Heidegger offers a view of life as the Poem of Being, calling for the homecoming for the human essence, an ethic of non-exploitative relation to the earth and to each other. An excellent example is Robert Mugerauer's application of Heidegger to issues in environmentalist ethics (Mugerauer 1995: 109ff; see also McWhorter 1992). For 'left-Heideggerians' on the other hand, the potentially Edenic elements in Heidegger's work are of less interest than the force of Heideggerian *Destruction* as a basis for a fundamental social critique, deeply critical of given thinking and institutions.

Heidegger's work made up a crucial part of the deeply critical reevaluation of the nature of Western history and thinking which characterized the second half of the twentieth century. Heidegger has been one of the major thinkers of what we now term globalization. The 1960s saw the emergence of ambitious readings of Western thought as a whole that owe much to Heidegger's (and to Nietzsche's) example. Michel

Foucault acknowledged Heidegger as, for him, 'always ... the essential philosopher' (quoted in Kritzman 1988: 250). Heidegger's 'history of being' became Foucault's conception of the history of Western thought as one of changing 'epistemes'. He was reacting against models of intellectual history as one of a continuously unfolding 'development', according to which, say, seventeenth-century biology can be understood as a cruder version of theories that emerged more clearly in that discipline in the eighteenth and subsequent centuries. Foucault argued that we must recognize alterations from one epoch to another in the most basic conceptions of what knowledge is, changes so profound as to render inquiry at one time incommensurable with work in the 'same' field at another (see Spanos 1993: 132–80). Thus nineteenth-century biology really has a deeper kinship with, for instance, nineteenth-century philology than with eighteenth-century biology, so drastically different have become the varying 'epistemes' or models of what knowledge itself is across the centuries. Heidegger was also an early influence on the revisionist Marxism of the so-called Frankfurt School, especially the work of Herbert Marcuse (1898–1979) (McCarthy 1993: 83–96).

Despite the vast indirect influence of Heidegger's thinking, however, can it be assimilated to oppositional cultural politics quite so easily as some defenders wish (e.g. Spanos 1993)? For instance, though Heidegger's criticism of the oppression latent in modern concepts of knowledge was supremely important for Foucault's later thinking about power and institutions and hence, indirectly, for much work influenced by Foucault in the literary academy (the so called 'new historicism' for example), there is much in this work that Heidegger would have found nihilistic, justifying perhaps his general disdain for literary criticism. A dominant assumption in almost all critical readings of today is that to unearth the cultural politics of a text is to reach the bottom line of a possible analysis. But that, for Heidegger, is nihilism, the reduction of the poetic to a function of competing claims to power or authority in human culture. It is to posit that nothing is more fundamental than the rivalry of human representations, the struggle of competing individuals or groups.

Work that transmits the most challenging side of Heidegger's thought cannot rest at that point. It is that which keeps open the possibility that its text is not just a production of the debates of its day, object for our interpretation, but that it makes a claim upon us, i.e. it concerns the truth of our existence in some sense.

So Heidegger's legacy is striking for its multiplicity and deep ambivalence. His attack on the anthropocentrism of Western thought aligns him with the deep ecology movement, its rejection of the attitude to the earth and its creatures as a mere resource, and which sees even space in terms (ludicrously) of 'conquest'. Heidegger's work is, in the title of one of the best books about him, *The Song of the Earth* (Haar 1993). At the same time many people are uneasy at the way Heidegger seems oddly blind to the contemporary world except as an intensification of decline. He seems uninterested in the diverse nature of modernity, taking its science, its individualism, its crimes and its achievements as undifferentiated instances of productionist metaphysics. There has also been disquiet about the way the very profundity of Heidegger's thinking, its intense focus only on 'essential' questions, leads to the dismissal as 'inessential' of many issues that yet matter deeply to many people – where in Heidegger is there to be found a sustained discussion of human relationships engaged with, say, issues of social justice, the family, sexual difference, childhood, love etc.?

The question of sexual difference is especially challenging. Heidegger argues that he is writing about so fundamental a level of being that one can say that *Dasein* has no gender. If, however, a counter-argument were to prevail that sexuality is perhaps primordial to the way a world is disclosed to anyone, then the issue would have to be reopened. To put it crudely, if the sexes have lived in different worlds, if only partially, then what could be more *geschichtlich* than that (see Derrida 1983)? Even Heidegger's pupil, Hans Georg Gadamer came to write that what is needed 'is not the persistent asking of ultimate questions, but the sense of what is feasible, what possible, what is correct, here and now' (Gadamer 1975: xxv). There has been a general recognition of both (1) the need to leave the intensely anti-modern moral climate of Heidegger's thinking and yet (2) to avoid lapsing back into thinking that is merely pre-Heideggerian.

AMERICAN HEIDEGGER: THE ROMANTIC 'POST-STRUCTURALIST'?

Uncritical admiration marked the first wave of literary criticism in English to look to Heidegger in the early 1970s.

Work of the early 1970s never formed a school and soon died off or merged into a second wave of work influenced by Derrida and Paul de Man. In retrospect the limitations of the early studies using Heidegger are clear, not least the fact that most of them referred to *Being and Time* rather than Heidegger's later work on the poetic. One feature was the tendency to use selected pieces of Heidegger's text to back up claims for the importance of specific poets, almost always poets in the tradition of twentieth-century American modernism, as in Paul Bové's *Destructive Poetics: Heidegger and Modern American Poetry* (1980), Joseph Riddel's book about William Carlos Williams (Riddell 1974), or Thomas J. Hines's study of Wallace Stevens (Hines 1976). Others seized on the way Heidegger's texts provide a defence of poetic language. Heidegger's distinction between ordinary instrumental language and poetic, revelatory language was easily assimilated to a criticism that continued the modernist agenda of a drive towards a purified, essential language with unique truth-bearing properties. In Gerald Bruns's early study, *Modern Poetry and the Idea of Language: A Critical and Historical Study* (1974), Heidegger's work was assimilated to a distinction between what is termed the 'Hermetic' and the 'Orphic' as modes of language. This opposition works ahistorically to demarcate two poles in Western poetics, the one, (the Hermetic) a reflexive concern with the density of language itself as a site of mystery, and the other (the Orphic) with language in its force of disclosure, its relation not to itself but to a world.

In effect these American studies of the 1970s developed the campaign of dominant critical school in the first three decades after the Second World War, that of the so-called New Critics, with their unphilosophical, romantic programme of celebrating poetic language as offering the reader a kind of unalienated subjective experience in which thought and feeling are organically bound together, a subjective 'enactment' or 'embodiment' of a thinking at odds with the abstract reductions of scientism.

POSTSTRUCTURALISM

Poststructuralism is usually presented in introductions to literary theory as an intellectual movement of the late 1960s and the 1970s. It is described as taking over and radicalizing certain ideas of the linguistics of Ferdinand de Saussure (1857–1913) and the method of research he had influenced (Structuralism). Thus Saussure had argued that the signs in a language are completely 'arbitrary' (i.e. not natural) in the way they possess meaning

– there is no inherent relation between the word 'home' and the thing or concept it refers to. What it means depends entirely on how that particular set of letters or sounds (h-o-m-e) functions in the system of language distinct from the functioning of other sets of letters or sounds. 'Post-structuralism' is presented as an argument that pushes this insight one step further. It argues that, for example, since a word in a language can only be explained in relation to other words, and so on, all methods of inter-preting a text that aim to pin it to some stable reference in the real world or to an author's meaning are doomed, that the critic is imprisoned in the unstable play of language.

This argument was falsely attributed to the thinking of Jacques Derrida. The work of Michel Foucault, of the critic Roland Barthes (1915–80) and of the psychoanalyst Jacques Lacan (1901–81) have all been presented as 'poststructuralist' at some time or other and similar simplistic arguments attributed to them.

In fact, however, 'Poststructuralism' in this sense barely ever existed. The idea that 'poststructuralism' was an intellectual movement is a self-perpetuating fabrication of journalistic 'introductions' to literary theory, too lazy to look at the diverse set of primary texts.

Heidegger's work also enabled critics take up the kind of 'anti-humanist' position on the agenda in structuralist and emergent 'post-structuralist' criticism at this time, i.e. attacking the view that human consciousness be seen as the final source of meaning in either language or history. Heidegger seemed to offer a position that could reconcile such anti-humanism with a defence of the uniqueness of the poetic. One culmination of this period of interest was a special edition of the journal, *boundary2*, (later a book) devoted to Heidegger and literature and edited by William Spanos, a Greek American Heideggerian who continued to defend the value of reading Heidegger through the 1970s, 1980s and 1990s (Spanos 1976).

Inevitably perhaps, given the strangeness of Heidegger's work, such studies assimilated it too strongly to intellectual positions already avail-able – generally to a Romantic and modernist tradition which cham-pions the poetic work in terms of the vague superiority of poetic truth, all couched at a level of generality that deprived the argument of specific historical force. The result rendered Heideggerian poetics a tamely European form of Zen, with just the kind of slant – loosely anti-commercial, anti-industrial, and anti-science – already so congenial to literary critics, oblivious in some cases of the oddness of celebrating how poetry 'founds' a world in the context of the Cold War and fighting in Vietnam. One would not guess from these readings that Heidegger is the thinker of the decline and probable death of art. In short, in effect, for all his criticism of aesthetics, Heidegger became the source of a new aestheticism.

A problem with almost all Heidegger-inspired readings of some chosen writer, from the 1970s till today, is that they take an argument about art from Heidegger's texts with often no regard for the very notion, that of the history of being, that gave them their critical, anti-modern edge. For instance, many appropriations of Heidegger read as if the characteristics he reserves to great art, such as that of the Greeks, could be simply claimed for modern art, without regard to the whole question of the death of art.

HERMENEUTICS

A more enduring legacy has been the total reconstruction of the discipline of hermeneutics (the art and theory of the interpretation of texts) in terms dominated by Heidegger's thinking. Here the major names are Hans-Georg Gadamer (1900–) and Paul Ricoeur (1913–).

Heidegger's general effect on the thought of the second half of the twentieth century was often to induce a 'hermeneutic turn,' i.e. a new concern with the nature and finitude of all acts of interpretation affected such diverse areas as anthropology, law studies, debates about cognitive science (as we have seen) and, of course, literary studies. In each case there has been a reexamination of not just the attainability but the desirability of ideals of objectivity that had previously been dominant. One example of this shift in the field of criticism has been a concern with the kind of often sub-conscious and untheorized interpretation that takes place in the very reading of a text, as in the so-called Reception Theory of Hans Robert Jauss and Wolfgang Iser which developed in Germany from the late 1960s (see Holub 1984). Reading is not some immediate process like seeing or sensing what is in text, but a deeply mediated set of interpretative skills – one reason that reading literature takes time to learn. Such work owed a great deal also to Hans Georg Gadamer's classic *Truth and Method* (1960) which was the first work to develop a general 'hermeneutics', or theory of interpretation, on the basis of Heidegger's work. Gadamer wrote: 'Heidegger's temporal analytics of human existence (*Dasein*) has, I think, shown convincingly that understanding is not just one of the various possible behaviours of the subject, but the mode of being of There-being [*Dasein*] itself . . . and hence includes the whole of its experience of the world' (Gadamer 1975: xviii). Gadamer was writing at time when, as now, the humanities were under intense pressure to model themselves on the natural sciences, to accept the latter as the only fully acceptable mode of knowledge. Against this, Gadamer stresses the way Heidegger's work on the essentially pre-reflective nature of human understanding endorses the authority of traditional intellectual skills, such as textual interpretation, without accepting the need to underwrite them with some more fully transparent 'scientific' method (even if such were possible). Gadamer also develops the crucial argument of 'The Origin of the Work of Art' that a work is not just to be seen as an expression of the views and values of its author, or of its time, but as engaging still with the question of truth. In other words, art cannot be relegated to the realms of the traditionally historical or merely subjective without making an arrogant restriction of the kind of claim it may make on us.

For Ricoeur, following Gadamer, we can no longer define hermeneutics or the theory of interpretation 'in terms of the search for the psychological intentions of another person which are concealed *behind* the text, and if we do not want to reduce interpretation to the dismantling of structures, then what remains to be interpreted?' (Ricoeur 1981: 141). The answer is a Heideggerian one: the interpreter should aim to inhabit and understand the mode of being projected by the text, i.e. a world in the sense given in the first chapter of this study:

> For what must be interpreted in a text is a *proposed world* which I could inhabit and wherein I could project one of my ownmost possibilities. This is what I call the world of the text, the world proper to *this* unique text.
>   . . . Through fiction and through poetry, new possibilities of being-in-the-world are opened up within everyday reality.
>
> (Ricoeur 1981: 142)

The reader's task is to submit, thoughtfully, to the terms of the text, but the ultimate goal, for Ricoeur is that mode of understanding which he terms 'appropriation'. The reader engages in an interaction between his or her 'world' and that of the text, with the goal of the 'convergence of the *world* horizons of the writer and the reader' (p. 192). The goal of interpretation becomes not the reconstitution of some dubious 'original' meaning but an elucidation of one's own world through the encounter with that of an other.

A striking difference between Ricoeur and Heidegger is the absence of anything equivalent to Heidegger's concept of the 'earth' in Ricoeur's argument, that resistant, inchoate element of the work in its otherness, irreducible to the cultural terms of being part of a 'world'. The work, as a site of the strife of 'world' and 'earth' cannot be seen simply as the projection of a world. As we saw in Chapter 3 (the example of why literary texts cannot have an index) Heidegger is fascinated by that element of the work that resists appropriation, that cannot be stabilized by interpretation, or made compatible with the work of worldly meaning. Gerald Bruns writes, against Ricoeur:

> The work is uncontainable within the world, resistant to its reasons, excessive with regard to the boundary that separates world from earth. The paradox of the work of art is that there is no place for it in the world it works to establish. Its sort of speaking, its words, cannot be made sense of in worldly terms.
>
> (Bruns 1993: 31)

Whereas Heidegger affirms the singularity of the work of art as an irreducibly strange mode of being, Ricoeur's project, Bruns argues, remains aligned with the major programme of poetics since Aristotle, namely of poetics as a subset of philosophy whose task is the full comprehension or appropriation of the poetic object.

BLANCHOT, DERRIDA AND DECONSTRUCTION

Bruns's criticisms of Ricoeur instantiate a major and continuing effect of Heidegger in contemporary literary study, a stress on the finitude of understanding and interpretation and an engagement with the issue of what in a text may be incompatible with notions of elucidation, comprehension or interpretation in the first place. It was initially in France that this side of Heidegger's work, the thought of the 'earth' so to speak, has had the most impact, especially in the thought and writing of Maurice Blanchot and Jacques Derrida.

The reworking of Heideggerian thinking on the poetic in the work of Blanchot and Derrida might be also termed a thought of the earth (not a phrase they use, though it may be useful here), sometimes against aspects of Heidegger's texts. Both these thinkers, however, are working within a broadly Heideggerian understanding of their context, conceived as that of Western thought as a whole, its deepest assumptions and repressions, and its suppression of what is other to it. Blanchot, who encountered Heidegger's work most fully in the 1950s, adapts and revises it in relation to his life-long fascination by the literary. Blanchot's *The Space of Literature* (1955) is marked everywhere by the reading of 'The Origin of the Work of Art':

> The statue glorifies the marble. . . . And the poem likewise is not made with ideas, or with words; it is the point from which words begin to become their appearance, and the *elemental depth* upon which this appearance is opened while at the same time it closes.

> (Blanchot 1982a: 223)

This earthly element of the work, however, is for Blanchot the primary one. The work is no longer, as it was for Heidegger, the mutual affirmation of world and earth in their constitutive antagonism (as we saw in Chapter 3). For Blanchot, the work does not enter, except by violent misappropriation, into the world's space, i.e. the realm of meaning, disclosure, cultural debate and truth. It remains with the darkness of the earth. Blanchot affirms in the poetic, the 'literary space', an anarchic acultural force that is never fully reducible to meaning nor capable of even the self-identity of an object, but which makes up a perpetual outside to history and the work of meaning. This is, among other things, a refusal in Heidegger of every thought of art as a possible 'homecoming' or retrieval of the human relation of being. Art remains, for Blanchot, a 'limit experience', a space of radical exile from culture and history. The poet is essentially a 'wanderer'. There is surely an implicit criticism of elements of Heidegger's Hölderlin readings here, their spiritual politics and romantic nationalism. Art for Blanchot is inherently a refusal of the historical place (the *polis*) of a specific people: '[the poet] belongs to the foreign, to the outside which knows no intimacy or limit, and to the separation which Hölderlin names when in his madness he sees rhythm's infinite space' (Blanchot 1982a: 237).

Derrida's name has already come up in this study several times as the most famous contemporary reader of Heidegger. A French Algerian of Jewish descent, Derrida's interest in the peculiar mode of being of the literary work of art led him in the 1950s to a deeply critical engage-ment with phenomenology, the particular school of twentieth-century philosophy from which Heidegger's work had earlier emerged. Heidegger then became a crucial reference for Derrida in the 1960s as he developed his own radical 'deconstruction' of the major texts and modes of thought that have defined the West since the Greeks. 'De-construction', often wildly misappropriated and distorted, then became the title for a mode of literary critical reading powerful throughout the 1970s and 1980s, especially in the over professionalized American academy. Simplistic views of 'deconstruction' as claiming, for example, that texts have no meaning, or that the critic's task is simply to affirm the text's vague strangeness in refusing to be pinned down and such like, all gave Derrida a kind of academic super-star status at odds with the challenging meticulous work he was in fact doing, often in Hei-degger's wake. (Such might have been Heidegger's fate perhaps, had he been born a generation later.) Although Derrida is too critical of Heidegger to be called simply a 'post-Heideggerian', this term is a far less misleading epithet for his work than that of 'poststructuralist' still sometimes heard in less scholarly work in literary theory.

Derrida's deconstruction of Western thought is the most prominent legatee of Heideggerian destruction/deconstruction. Both thinkers take received modes of philosophizing and thought to their limits, not to affirm a blandly fashionable relativism, but to shake up the deepest assumptions of Western thought, opening it to what other modes of being and thinking, if any, might be conceived beside it. For both, the singular mode of being of the literary is crucial to this venture.

Coming to Derrida the phrase 'After Heidegger' becomes even more problematic. One thing that Derrida, like Foucault, takes from the reading of Heidegger is a deconstruction of received ideas of intellectual history. So, rather than speak in familiar ways about 'Heidegger's influ-ence' on Derrida it would be more accurate to speak of Heidegger's works having a plural and heterogeneous series of affects in the work of Derrida and others. Heidegger's work is not some monolith to be judged and labelled, as if we had somehow got beyond it. We are speaking of diverse texts with plural and contradictory effects, some at odds with each other.

Derrida's reading of Western thought since the Greeks as domi-nated by what he terms 'logocentrism' is effectively Heidegger's point about the determination of being as presence. However, his practice of close reading, though close to Heidegger's, does not attribute to metaphysical modes of thinking the kind of all-pervasive dominance which Heidegger often does when dealing with a text from the tradition. Derrida's gives attention to apparently trivial or marginal elements in a text – something in a footnote or some casual example – in order to show up the continual instability of dominant ways of reading:

> The norms of minimal intelligibility are not absolute and ahistorical, but merely more stable than others. They depend upon socio-institutional conditions, hence upon non-natural relations of power that by essence are mobile and founded upon complex conventional structures that in principle may be analyzed, deconstructed, and transformed; and, in fact, these structures are in the process of transforming themselves profoundly and, above all, very rapidly . . . 'deconstruction' is firstly this destabilization on the move.
>
> (Derrida 1988: 147)

Derrida sees elements in Heidegger's reading that restrain this process of transformation in ways that need to be analysed or criticized. So it seems, at first, that Derrida turns Heidegger against Heidegger: 'I attempt to locate in Heidegger's thought . . . the signs of a belonging to metaphysics' (Derrida 1981: 10). Examples we have met already would include Heidegger's German chauvinism and his little examined view of 'the people' as the arena for the event of disclosure. In short what we would now call a hidden 'identity politics' marks Heidegger's thinking and sometimes affiliates it, despite itself, to metaphysical thinking.

Perhaps Heidegger did not resist the hubris of assuming one's own period to be the culminating crisis or the climax of history, the one which gives the key to reading all the others. For Derrida, however, deep history (*Geschichte*) is far more complex than Heidegger's narrative of the gradual subjection of being would imply; it is more ambiguous, multi-layered and characterized by multiple rifts, tensions and contradictions. He writes, against Heidegger, that 'although an epoch [in Heidegger's history of being] is not a historiological period, it is still a large ensemble or totality gathered toward a single sense', that of the intensifying oblivion of being (Derrida 1987: 174). Fixation upon this single sense renders Heidegger insensitive at times to the heterogeneity of the history of thought. The seventeenth-century thinker Baruch de Spinoza (1632–77) for instance, shows almost none of the key traits that Heidegger asserts characterize his and our epoch: Spinoza's, writes Derrida, is 'a thought that is not of the subject, not of representedness, not of sufficient reason, not of certitude, not of finalism': Heidegger largely ignores Spinoza (Derrida 1987: 172).

One of the most definitive characteristics of metaphysics Derrida describes as follows:

All metaphysicians, from Plato to Rousseau, Descartes to Husserl, have proceeded in this way, conceiving good to be before evil, the positive before the negative, the pure before the impure, the simple before the complex, the essential before the accidental, the imitated before the imitation, etc. And this is not just one metaphysical gesture among others, it is the metaphysical exigency, that which has been the most constant, most profound and most potent.

(Derrida 1988: 93)

This account also touches on Heidegger. Heidegger acknowledges the necessity of both meditative thinking and of calculative modes of rationality: 'There are, then, two kinds of thinking, each justified and needed in its own way' (D: 46). In practice, however, 'calculative' reasoning, as it is removed from the exclusive privilege which the West has tended to give it, is often severely caricatured. A distinction between the essential and non-essential is still working in what Derrida describes as a 'metaphysical' way in the rhetorical strategies of many of Heidegger's texts, setting up an exclusionist agenda which places a lot of issues as merely secondary, derivative or superficial in relation to the deep issues. We must consider if there is too purist a drive in Heidegger's thinking of a non-appropriative relation to being. 'Heidegger avers that the essence of technology is nothing technological: his thinking of technology *as such* and *as an essence* tries in a classically philosophical manner to shelter the thought and language of essence from contamination' (Derrida 1987: 172). Similar points can be made about such Heideggerian claims as that the sciences 'are not thinking' (WT: 33) but are merely a secondary technique of ratiocination, or Heidegger's reaffirmation of a difference of essence between the human and the animal. With critique of this kind, pushing Heidegger's arguments with traditional categories of thought against such elements lingering in his own work, Derrida's writings remain Heidegger's most potent legacy, most faithful to Heidegger's work in its very unfaithfulness to it.

Derrida's work takes up Heidegger's criticisms of received ways of thinking about the poetic. Derrida's thoughts on reading literature, as in his lucid interview with Derek Attridge, offer what can be seen as a partial and responsible formalization of Heideggerian reading (Derrida 1992: 33–75). Derrida stresses the irreducibility of the literary to the dominant assumptions which literary criticism has taken over from metaphysics: the way the very mode of being of the literary or poetic resists being studied from the outside like some sort of object but challenges dominant philosophical assumptions about the being of anything; the inadequacy of reading for the content; the reductiveness of received ideas of historical context, and of assumptions about the very idea of interpretation as the finding of a 'meaning'; the irreducible singularity of the work and the demands this singularity makes on the reader, on the place of the reader in the determining what force the work may have; the tensions between literature and traditional institutions of intellectual authority and learning (such as the university) . . . and so on. Derrida's enigmatic but fascinating prose poem, 'Che cos'è la poesia?' (Derrida 1991: 221–37) celebrates the poetic as a fragile singularity of language, 'humble, close to the earth' (231–3), vulnerable to obliteration by the very commonalty of the medium, language, it which it can alone appear.

Derrida's concern with a certain purism in Heidegger's thought also leads him to qualify an element of idealization of the poetic in Heidegger. Thus, although Derrida endorses the critical and deconstructive force of Heidegger's readings, we are led to qualify the redemptive side of Heidegger's turn to the poetic. One issue here concerns Heidegger's idea of a reading of the poetic which, in response to the singularity of the work before it, would aim finally to disappear as a commentary: '[T]he elucidating speech', writes Heidegger (as we saw in Chapter 6), 'must each time shatter itself and what it had attempted to do' and 'The last, but also the most difficult step of every interpretation, consists in its disappearing before the pure presence of the poem' (E: 22). But could there ever be such a thing as 'the pure presence of the poem'? Does not Heidegger's postulate that there could be risk falling foul of the very criticisms he makes himself of the vulgar notion that there is such a thing as a Sophocles work 'in itself' or Kant 'in itself' (see p. 95 of this study)? Such works do not have the mode of being of objects, but more that of events whose efficacy and force alter – or may be stifled by – the world in which they are being read?

The act of interpretation or commentary is thus not some sort of accident that befalls the pure presencing of the text, as Heidegger already recognizes himself in his notion that the reader's or spectator's 'preservation' is essential to the work-being of the work of art. Instead, 'commentary, 'reading' and 'elucidation' have to be accepted as structurally inherent to the very appearance, or legibility, of a work, however uncomfortable this may to any reader dreaming of securing the text as an unchallengeable anchor to their reading. Derrida's thinking on the literary (after Blanchot 1993: 389ff) repeatedly refuses the idea of the self-sufficient unity of the work implicit in such idealizations (see Derrida 1992: 48). The being of the literary is thus for Derrida and Blanchot a contaminated one, resistant to the kind of purist distinction Heidegger makes between *Dichtung* and 'mere' 'literature'. For instance, Shakespeare's *Henry V* can be read, with evidence amassed in detail on both sides, both as the celebration of an ideal monarch and the hero of Agincourt it appears to be, *and* as the ironizing presentation of such a figure and the kinds of language associated with him, bringing out the way he builds and imposes an images of himself. Many of Blake's songs of innocence, with their childish speakers, can be read 'straight' as expressions of a sentimental Christianity *or* as ironic stagings of such views. Exactly the same sequence of words can be subjected, in effect, to opposite interpretations with equal justification! This might make one question the plausibility of placing the poetic at the heart of a redemptive rather than simply critical cultural programme, even in so sophisticated a way as Heidegger's meditations on *Dichtung*. Poetic language may be irreducible to productionist thinking, but it also brings with it, necessarily, a potential destabilization of the institution of all serious values.

So, how does Derrida's reading affect the issue of judging Heidegger's importance? To criticize Heidegger as Derrida does, in terms of certain 'signs of a belonging to metaphysics' is still the opposite of refuting him, for it is forces in Heidegger's own thinking that are being brought to bear against him. Who, after all, is responsible for the argument that Western metaphysics must be deconstructed but Heidegger? Work such as Heidegger's which also provides the source of most of the thinking one might want to direct against that work – this is not something anyone is going to be able to view from the 'outside' for a very long time.

FURTHER READING

WORKS BY HEIDEGGER

For reading Heidegger's own texts, there is little alternative to jumping
in at the deep end, especially for those with little or no sense of philosophy. The following selected texts may be a useful first point of call.
The two sections below are listed in what seems an approximate order
of difficulty.

GENERAL

'The Age of the World Picture,' in *The Question Concerning Technology*,
trans. William Lovitt, New York: Harper, 1977, pp. 115–54.

'Only a God Can Save us,' trans. Maria P. Alter and John Caputo,
Philosophy Today 20 (1976), pp. 267–85; reproduced in Richard Wolin
ed., *The Heidegger Controversy*, Cambridge Massachusetts; London: MIT
Press, 1993, pp. 91–116.

Heidegger's posthumously published interview with *Der Spiegel*
contains his account of the events of 1933–4 and also a general take
on his life's work.

What is Philosophy? [1955], trans. William Kluback and Jean T. Wilde, Plymouth: Vision Press, 1989.

A brief and relatively accessible lecture.

The Fundamental Concepts of Metaphysics: World, Finitude, Solitude [1983: lecture course of 1929–30], trans. William McNeill and Nicholas Walker, Bloomington and Indianapolis: Indiana University Press, 1992.

Good example of Heidegger's detailed attention to the fundamental issues implicit in even the most ordinary experience (boredom, in this case).

The Principle of Reason [1957], trans. Reginald Lilly, Bloomington and Indianapolis: Indiana University Press, 1991.

Being and Time [1927], trans. John Macquarrie and Edward Robinson, Oxford: Blackwell, 1962.

Not an easy read, but too important to be omitted. Becomes far more relaxed in pace after Heidegger's Introduction. Refer also to the guides by Dreyfus, Steiner, Rée or Wood (see below).

ART, POETRY, LANGUAGE

Hölderlin's Hymns 'Germanien' and 'Der Rhein'.

A translation by William McNeill is currently in preparation, to appear from Indiana University Press. These were Heidegger's earliest lectures on the poetic and remain the most accessible.

Elucidations of Hölderlin's Poetry [4th edn 1971], trans. Keith Hoeller, Amherst, NY: Humanity Books, 2000.

Heidegger's greatest work on poetics. The first two essays are the most accessible.

Poetry, Language, Thought, trans. Albert Hofstadter, New York, NY: Harper & Row, 1971.

Contains 'The Origin of the Work of Art', and other papers. Hofstadter's translation of 'The Origin of the Work of Art' also appears in *Philosophies of Art and Beauty: Selected Readings in Aesthetics from Plato to Heidegger*, ed. Albert Hofstadter and Richard Kuhns, Chicago: University of Chicago Press, 1976.

On the Way to Language [1957], trans. Peter D. Hertz, San Francisco, Ca.: Harper & Row, 1971.

A collection of papers on the nature of language, including the marvellous 'A Dialogue on Language: between a Japanese and an Inquirer'.

Gedachtes/Thoughts [1971], trans. Keith Hoeller, *Philosophy Today* 20 (1976), pp. 286–91.

A series of Heidegger's 'poems'.

THE *GESAMTAUSGABE*

A full bibliography of the *Gesamtausgabe*, or Complete Works, to date, in German and in translation, is updated yearly in the journal *Heidegger Studies*. But see also Theodor Kisiel, 'Heidegger's *Gesamtausgabe*: An International Scandal of Scholarship', *Philosophy Today* 31 (1995), pp. 3–15.

Inwood (1999) can be used as a basic index to Heidegger's work in German and English translation.

WORKS ON HEIDEGGER

BIOGRAPHIES

Hugo Ott (1993) *Martin Heidegger: A Political Life*, trans. Allan Blunden, New York: Basic Books; London: HarperCollins.

The reliable book on Heidegger, Nazism, and Heidegger's shabby academic politics.

Heinrich Wiegand Petzet (1993) *Encounters and Dialogues with Martin Heidegger 1929–1976*, trans. Parvis Emad and Kenneth Maly, Chicago: University of Chicago Press.

Informal and very readable episodes of biography from a disciple who seems to have genuinely loved Heidegger.

Rüdiger Safranski (1998). *Martin Heidegger: Between Good and Evil*, trans. Ewald Osers, Cambridge Mass.: Harvard University Press.

A very well paced general biography.

INTERNET

The 'Ereignis' site at http://www.webcom.com/~paf/ereignis.html

This mainly provides helpful bibliographies of studies of Heidegger in relation to specific fields or issues, e.g. Heidegger and the Environment, Heidegger and Science, and so on.

INTRODUCTORY LEVEL (GENERAL)

David Cooper (1996) *Thinkers of Our Time: Heidegger*, London: The Claridge Press.

With Rée (1998) this is the clearest of the several available introductions to Heidegger. It is focused, like the others, on *Being and Time*.

Hubert L. Dreyfus (1985) 'Holism and Hermeneutics', in Robert Hollinger ed., *Hermeneutics and Praxis*, Notre Dame, Indiana: University of Notre Dame Press, pp. 227–47.

Read this if you are still feeling stuck about Heidegger's main arguments. There is little on literature directly, but the issues covered are those described in Chapter 1 of the present introduction.

Hubert L. Dreyfus (1991) *Being-in-the-World: A Commentary on Heidegger's* Being and Time, Division 1, Cambridge Mass.: Harvard University Press.

Lucid, step by step philosophical introduction. The value of Dreyfus's work lies in the way that he does not write as an uncritical disciple whose aims are limited to getting at the master's meaning, or in Heidegger's kind of language. He tries to clarify what Heidegger's arguments are, then considers their strengths, weaknesses and implications.

Hubert L. Dreyfus, and Stuart E. Dreyfus (1986) *Mind over Machine: The Power of Human Intuition and Expertise in the Era of the Computer*, Oxford: Basil Blackwell.

Not on Heidegger directly but a case of Heideggerian thinking at work. If you are still feeling stuck at the most basic level, look at the 'Prologue' to this book or the Dreyfus article 'Holism and Hermeneutics'.

Reinhard May (1996) *Heidegger's Hidden Sources*, London: Routledge.

Heidegger's massive unacknowledged debt to Taoist and Buddhist thought?

Robert Mugerauer (1995) *Interpreting Environments: Tradition, Deconstruction, Hermeneutics*, Austin: University of Texas Press.

Lucid work on Heidegger and environmental ethics, with a useful reference to further reading on Heidegger and the deep ecology movement (p. 155).

Robert Mugerauer (1988) *Heidegger's Language and Thought*, Atlantic Highlands, NJ: Humanities Press.

Especially clear and useful on Heidegger and language, and on Heidegger's experiments with the dialogue form as a mode of disciplined thinking other than the traditional procedures of analysis or system building.

Polt Richard (1999) *Heidegger*, London: UCL Press.

Another fairly accessible introduction, slightly longer than Cooper (1996) but just as clear, meant primarily for beginning students in philosophy. Goes slightly further into the later Heidegger than other introductions.

Jonathan Rée (1998) *Heidegger*. London: Phoenix.

A snappy, lucid little book on *Being and Time*.

George Steiner (1991) *Martin Heidegger*, Chicago: University of Chicago Press.

A revised version of a long-popular introduction from the Modern Masters series, first published in 1978, focused mostly on *Being and Time*. A new introduction concentrates helpfully on the cultural context of Heidegger in the Germany of the first forty years of the twentieth century and also surveys the latest controversy, post-1987, on Heidegger and Nazism.

Julian Young (1997). *Heidegger, Philosophy, Nazism*, Cambridge: Cambridge University Press.

Unusually lucid, a thorough defence of Heidegger, but also very readable as an account of his thought in general. Much should be accessible to students unfamiliar with philosophy.

Michael E. Zimmerman (1990) *Heidegger's Confrontation with Modernity: Technology, Politics, Art*, Bloomington: Indiana University Press.

Lucid, especially clear on the cultural context of Heidegger's thinking in the 1930s and the role art played in Heidegger's 'spiritual' politics. Further discussion of this book can be found in Chapter 7 of the present study.

OTHER (GENERAL)

David Carroll (1990) Foreword to Jean François Lyotard, *Heidegger and 'the Jews'*, trans. Andreas Michel and Mark Roberts, Minneapolis, London: University of Minnesota Press, pp. vii–xxix.

Useful for introducing the debate on Heidegger's silence about the holocaust.

Simon Critchley (1999) 'Black Socrates? Questioning the Philosophical Tradition', in *Ethics Politics Subjectivity*, London: Verso, pp. 122–42.

This is not explicitly on Heidegger, but concerns the myths the philosophical tradition has constructed about its Greek origins, its Eurocentrism and the notion of tradition itself. All these issues bear upon Heidegger.

Fred Dallmayr (1995) 'Heidegger and Freud', in Babette Babich (ed.) *From Phenomenology to Thought, Errancy, and Desire: Essays in Honor of William J. Richardson, S.J.*, Dordrecht: Kluwer Academic Publishers, 1995, pp. 547–65.

Indispensable on Heidegger's critical reading of psychoanalysis in his so-called Zollikon Seminars (a translations of these is due in 2001).

Parvis Emad (1992) 'Thinking more deeply into the question of translation: essential translation and the unfolding of language' in Christopher Macann (ed.) *Martin Heidegger: Critical Assessments*, 4 vols., London: Routledge, 1992, Vol. 3 'Language', pp. 58–78.

On Heidegger's thinking about and use of translation.

Michel Haar (1993) *The Song of the Earth: Heidegger and the Grounds of the History of Being*, trans. Reginald Lily, Bloomington: Indiana University Press.

Superb on the influential/radical notion of the 'earth' in Heidegger. Written at what might be termed an intermediate level of difficulty.

Michael Inwood (1999) *A Heidegger Dictionary,* Oxford: Blackwell.

Lists major issues and terms alphabetically. Relatively scanty on poetic issues, however. Can be used as a partial index to Heidegger's corpus.

David Kolb (1995) 'Raising Atlantis: The Later Heidegger and Contemporary Philosophy', in Babette Babich (ed.) *From Phenomenology to Thought, Errancy, and Desire: Essays in Honor of William J. Richardson, S.J.,* Dordrecht: Kluwer Academic Publishers, pp. 55–69.

Maps later Heidegger on to positions in contemporary analytic philosophy. Useful for students of analytic philosophy.

Philippe Lacoue-Labarthe (1990) *Heidegger, Art and Politics*, trans. Chris Turner, Oxford: Blackwell.

An influential if pretentiously written book on the controversy about Heidegger and Nazism, discussed in Chapter 7 of this study.

Christopher Macann, (ed.) (1992) *Martin Heidegger: Critical Assessments*, 4 vols, London: Routledge.

A large and invaluable critical anthology, covering most aspects of Heidegger's work. Intended mainly for philosophy students.

Alan Milchman and Alan Rosenberg (1996) *Martin Heidegger and the Holocaust*, Atlantic Heights, NJ · Humanities Press.

Useful if rather repetitive collection of essays on Heidegger's 'silence'.

Richard Wolin, (ed.) (1993) *The Heidegger Controversy: A Critical Reader,* Cambridge Massachusetts: MIT, pp. 29–39.

Invaluable collection of documents and essays relating to the Nazism controversy.

LITERARY AND CRITICAL TOPICS

INTRODUCTORY MATERIAL

Again, as most books written on Heidegger have an audience in philosophy in mind, there are few texts on Heidegger and literature that non-philosophers will find immediately easy to read (hence this present study!). The following suggest themselves as first ports of call.

Andrew Bowie (1997) 'Introduction: Reviewing the Theoretical Canon', in *From Romanticism to Critical Theory: The Philosophy of German Literary Theory*, London: Routledge, pp. 1–27.

Useful defence of the relevance of Heidegger's notion of truth in contemporary literary theory.

Gerald Bruns (1989) *Heidegger's Estrangements: Language, Truth, and Poetry*, New Haven: Yale University Press.

Lively and accessible lectures. Highly recommended, though Bruns omits much reference to the notion of the 'history of being'.

Gerald Bruns (1993) 'Against Poetry', in David E. Klemm and William Schweiker eds, *Meanings in Texts and Actions: Questioning Paul Ricoeur*, Charlottesville: University Press of Virginia, pp. 26–46.

A lucid, shortish paper which brings out the distinction between Heidegger's deconstructive understanding of poetry and the more appropriative thinking of Ricoeur's hermeneutics.

Gerald Bruns (1994) 'Martin Heidegger', in Michael Gordon and Martin Kreswirth eds, *The Johns Hopkins Guide to Literary Theory and Criticism*, Baltimore, Johns Hopkins University Press, pp. 73–75.

Very brief overview.

John D. Caputo (1993) *Demythologizing Heidegger*, Bloomington: Indiana University Press.

Lucid example of the 1990s' turn against Heidegger, especially against the notion of the 'history of being'. Contains an accessible but rather caricaturing chapter attacking Heidegger on the poetic ('Heidegger's Poets').

Timothy Clark (1997) 'Contradictory Passion: Inspiration in Blanchot's *The Space of Literature* (1995)', in Clark (1997), pp. 238–58.

Works step by step through Blanchot's influential revisionist version of Heidegger's argument in 'The Origin of the Work of Art'.

William V. Spanos (1993) *Heidegger and Criticism: Retrieving the Cultural Politics of Destruction*, Minneapolis: University of Minnesota Press.

Spanos has devoted most of intellectual career to Heidegger and literature. This book is a series of essays, written or revised with the post 1987 fascist controversy in mind. It reassesses and defends Heidegger as a thinker who can still inform a responsible oppositional criticism. Spanos is more interested in following through Heidegger's criticisms of received thinking than in the specifics of Heideggerian readings of Hölderlin and others.

Charles Taylor (1992) 'Heidegger, Language, and Ecology', [on language in general] in Hubert L. Dreyfus and Harrison Hall eds, *Heidegger: A Critical Reader*, Oxford: Blackwell, pp. 247–69.

Situates Heidegger's thinking on language in a specific intellectual tradition in a way that makes it much clearer.

Krzysztof Ziarek (1989) 'The Reception of Heidegger's Thought in American Literary Criticism', *Diacritics* 19, nos. 3–4, pp. 114–26.

Review article on the reception of Heidegger in American criticism of the 1970s and early 1980s (i.e. corresponding to that discussed on pages 142–5 in the subsection 'American Heidegger: The Romantic "Post-Structuralist"?').

OTHER (LITERARY AND CRITICAL TOPICS)

This lists material at what might be termed an intermediate level of difficulty.

Robert Bernasconi (1992) 'The transformation of language at another beginning', in Christopher Macann (ed.) *Martin Heidegger: Critical Assessments*, 3 vols., London and New York: Routledge, 1992, III, pp. 168–89.

Clear and accessible on issues of Derrida's relation to Heidegger and the status of language at the closure of the metaphysical tradition.

Timothy Clark (1992) *Derrida, Heidegger, Blanchot: Sources of Derrida's Notion and Practice of Literature*, Cambridge: Cambridge University Press.

Argues that Heidegger is the major impetus behind the kind of deconstructive questioning of literature found in Maurice Blanchot and Jacques Derrida, dissociating the latter's work from the journalistic catch-all term 'poststructuralism'.

Rodophe Gasché and Anthony Appiah eds (1989) 'Heidegger: Art and Politics', special double issue of *Diacritics* 19 (3–4).
    A varied collection of essays.

Arthur A. Grogan (1992) 'Questions from Heidegger's Hölderlin-Interpretations', *Philosophy Today* 36, pp. 114–21.
    Useful for those who have already been working on this issue, but not for beginnners.

David Halliburton (1981) *Poetic Thinking: An Approach to Heidegger*, Chicago and London: University of Chicago Press.
    A study of Heidegger's later work (i.e. post *Being and Time*), setting out its arguments clearly, though in a way that has the effect of down-playing the strangeness and challenge of the way in which Heidegger philosophizes. Still very useful, if slightly dated by new material that has become available since 1981.

Emmanuel Levinas (1987) 'Reality and its Shadow', in *Collected Philosophical Papers*, trans. Alphonso Lingis, Dordrecht: Martinus Nijhoff, pp. 1–13.
    Doesn't mention Heidegger's essay on art, but covers similar ground in a way implicitly critical of Heidegger.

Joseph D. Lewandowski (1994) 'Heidegger, literary theory and social criticism', *Philosophy and Social Criticism* 20, pp. 109–22.
    Review essay of Spanos, *Heidegger and Criticism*, sceptical of the extent to which Heidegger can be claimed as a source of emancipatory thought by Spanos and others.

John T. Lysaker (1993) 'Heidegger After the Fall'. *Research in Phenomenology* (23), pp. 201–11.
    Succinct and critical review article of Véronique Fóti's influential criticisms of Heidegger in her *Heidegger and the Poets* (1992).

William V. Spanos (ed.) (1976) *Martin Heidegger and the Question of Literature: Towards a Postmodern Literary Hermeneutics,* Bloomington: Indiana University Press.

Useful, if slightly out of date, with its focus mainly on the Heidegger of *Being and Time*.

WORKS CITED

Date of original publication, where applicable, is given in square brackets.

Babich, Babette (ed.) (1995) *From Phenomenology to Thought, Errancy, and Desire: Essays in Honor of William J. Richardson, S.J.*, Dordrecht: Kluwer Academic Publishers.

Bennington, Geoffrey (1994) *Legislations: The Politics of Deconstruction*, London: Verso.

Bernasconi, Robert (1985) *The Question of Language in Heidegger's History of Being*, Atlantic Highlands, NJ.: Humanities Press.

—— (1995) 'I Will Tell You Who You Are.' Heidegger on Greco-German Destiny and *Amerikanismus*, in Babette E. Babich (ed.) *From Phenomenology to Thought, Errancy, and Desire: Essays in Honor of William J. Richardson, S.J.*, Dordrecht: Kluwer, pp. 301–13.

Bernstein, J. M. (1992) *The Fate of Art: Aesthetic Alienation from Kant to Derrida and Adorno*, Cambridge: Polity Press.

Blanchot, Maurice (1959) 'L'attente', in Gunter Neske (ed.) *Martin Heidegger zum Siebzigsten Geburtstag*, Pfullingen, Neske, pp. 217–24.

—— (1962) *L'attente, L'oubli*, Paris: Gallimard.

—— (1993) *The Infinite Conversation* [1969], Minneapolis: University of Minnesota Press.

—— (1982a) *The Space of Literature* [1955], trans. Ann Smock, Lincoln Neb.: University of Nebraska Press.

—— (1982b) *The Sirens' Song: Selected Essays*, trans. Sacha Rabinovitch, Gabriel Josipovici (ed.), Sussex: Harvester.

Bové, Paul (1980) *Destructive Poetics: Heidegger and Modern American Poetry*, New York: Columbia University Press.

Breton, André (1988) *Oeuvres Complètes*, vol. I, Marguerite Bonnet (ed.), Paris: Gallimard.

Bruns, Gerald (1974) *Modern Poetry and the Idea of Language: A Critical and Historical Study*, New Haven: Yale University Press.

—— (1989) *Heidegger's Estrangements: Language, Truth, and Poetry*, New Haven: Yale University Press.

—— (1993) 'Against Poetry', in David E. Klemm and William Schweiker (eds) *Meanings in Texts and Actions: Questioning Paul Ricoeur*, Charlottesville: University Press of Virginia, pp. 26–46.

—— (1994) 'Martin Heidegger', in Michael Gordon and Martin Kreswirth (eds) *The Johns Hopkins Guide to Literary Theory and Criticism*, Baltimore, Johns Hopkins University Press, pp. 73–5.

Cahoone, Lawrence E. (ed.) (1996) *From Modernism to Postmodernism: An Anthology*, Oxford: Blackwell.

Caputo, John D. (1993) *Demythologizing Heidegger*, Bloomington: Indiana University Press.

Cascardi, Anthony J. (1992) *The Subject of Modernity*, Cambridge: Cambridge University Press.

Celan, Paul (1983) *Gesammelte Werke*, 5 vols, Beda Allemann and Stefan Reichert (eds), Frankfurt: Suhrkamp.

Clark, Timothy (1997) *The Theory of Inspiration: Composition as a Crisis of Subjectivity in Romantic and Post-Romantic Writing*, Manchester: Manchester University Press.

Cooper, David (1996) *Thinkers of Our Time: Heidegger*, London: The Claridge Press.

Constantine, David (1988) *Hölderlin*, Oxford: Clarendon Press.

Critchley, Simon (1999) 'Black Socrates? Questioning the Philosophical Tradition', in S. Critchley *Ethics Politics Subjectivity*, London: Verso, pp. 122–42.

Critical Inquiry (1989) Vol. 15, no. 2 Winter 1989. Special issue on Heidegger and Nazism.

Davies, Paul (1993) *The Mind of God: Science and the Search for Ultimate Meaning*, London: Penguin.

Derrida, Jacques (1981) *Positions*, trans, Alan Bass, Chicago: University of Chicago Press.

—— (1982) *Margins of Philosophy*, trans. Alan Bass, Chicago: University of Chicago Press.

—— (1983) 'Geschlecht: sexual difference, ontological difference', *Research in Phenomenology* 13, pp. 65–83.

—— (1987) 'On Reading Heidegger', *Research in Phenomenology*, 17, pp. 171–85.

—— (1988) *Limited Inc*, trans. Samuel Weber, Evanston Ill., Northwestern University Press.

—— (1989) *Of Spirit*, trans. Geoffrey Bennington and Rachel Bowlby, Chicago: University of Chicago Press.

—— (1991) 'Che cos'è la poesia?' trans. Peggy Kamuf, in *A Derrida Reader: Between the Blinds*, Kamuf (ed.), London and New York: Harvester Wheatsheaf, pp. 221–37.

—— (1992) 'This Strange Institution Called Literature', in Derek Attridge (ed.) *Acts of Literature*, London: Routledge, 1992, pp. 33–75.

—— (1995) *Points . . .: Interviews 1974–1994*, trans. Peggy Kamuf *et al.*, Elisabeth Weber (ed.), Stanford Ca., Stanford University Press.

—— (1998) *Of Grammatology*, trans. Gayatri Chakravorty Spivak, corr. edn. Baltimore: Johns Hopkins University Press.

—— (1999) 'Hospitality, justice and responsibility: a dialogue with Jacques Derrida', in Richard Kearney, Mark Dooley (eds), *Questioning Ethics: Contemporary Debates in Philosophy*, London: Routledge, pp. 65–83.

Dreyfus, Hubert L. (1981) 'From Micro-Worlds to Knowledge Representation: AI at an Impasse', in John Haugeland (ed.) *Mind Design: Philosophy, Psychology, Artificial Intelligence*, Cambridge Massachusetts: MIT, pp. 161–204.

—— (1985) 'Holism and Hermeneutics', in Robert Hollinger (ed.) *Hermeneutics and Praxis*, Notre Dame, Indiana: University of Notre Dame Press, pp. 227–47.

—— (1991) *Being-in-the-World: A Commentary on Heidegger's* Being and Time, Division 1, Cambridge, Mass.: Harvard University Press.

—— (1998) 'Philosophy of Artificial Intelligence: Response to My Critics', in Terrell Ward Bynumn and James H. Moor (eds) *The Digital Phoenix: How Computers are Changing Philosophy*, Oxford: Basil Blackwell, pp. 193–212.

Dreyfus, Hubert L. and Stuart E. Dreyfus (1986) *Mind over Machine: The Power of Human Intuition and Expertise in the Era of the Computer*, Oxford: Basil Blackwell.

Dreyfus, Hubert L. and Harrison Hall (eds) (1992) *Heidegger: A Critical Reader*, Oxford: Blackwell.

Emad, P. (1992) 'Thinking more deeply into the question of translation: essential translation and the unfolding of language' in Christopher Macann (ed.) *Martin Heidegger: Critical Assessments*, 4 vols, London: Routledge, 1992, Vol. 3 'Language' pp. 58–78.

Emmerich, Wolfgang (1998) *Paul Celan*, Hamburg: Rowolt.

Farias, Victor (1989) *Heidegger and Nazism* [1987], trans. Paul Burrell and Gabriel Ricci, Philadelphia, Pa.: Temple.

Fehrmann, Carl (1980) *Poetic Creation: Inspiration or Craft*, trans. Karin Petherick, Minneapolis: University of Minnesota Press.

Fóti, Véronique (1992) *Heidegger and the Poets: Poesis, Sophia, Techne*, London; New Jersey: Humanities Press.

—— (1998) 'Heidegger and "The Way of Art": the empty origin and contemporary abstraction', *Continental Philosophy Review* 31, pp. 337–51.

Gadamer, Hans-Georg (1975) *Truth and Method*, trans. William Glen-Doepel, London: Sheed and Ward.

—— (1985) *Philosophical Apprenticeships*, trans. Robert R. Sullivan, Boston: MIT Press.

Gadamer, Hans-Georg (1994) *Heidegger's Ways*, trans. John W. Stanley, Albany, NY: State University of New York Press.

Golb, J.D. (1988) 'Celan and Heidegger: A Reading of "Todtnauberg"', *Seminar: A Journal of Germanic Studies*, 24, pp. 255–67.

Haar, Michel (1993) *The Song of the Earth: Heidegger and the Grounds of the History of Being*, trans. Reginald Lily, Bloomington: Indiana University Press.

Hamilton, Paul (1996) *Historicism*. London: Routledge.

John Haugeland (1985) *Artificial Intelligence: The Very Idea*, Cambridge Massachusetts: MIT.

Hegel, G. W. F. (1993) *Introductory Lectures on Aesthetics*, trans. Bernard Bosonquet, Michael Inwood (ed.), London: Penguin.

Heidegger, Martin (1962) *Being and Time* [1927], trans. John Macquarrie and Edward Robinson. Oxford: Blackwell.

—— (1966) *Discourse on Thinking*, trans. John M. Anderson and E. Hans Freund, New York, NY: Harper & Row.

—— (1968) *What is Called Thinking* [1954], trans. J. Glenn Gray, New York, NY: Harper & Row.

(1971a) *Poetry, Language, Thought*, trans. Albert Hofstadter, New York, NY: Harper & Row.

—— (1971b) *On the Way to Language* [1957], trans. Peter D. Hertz, San Francisco, Ca.: Harper & Row.

—— (1972) *On Time and Being* [1969], trans. Joan Stambaugh, New York, NY: Harper and Row.

—— (1975a) *Early Greek Thinking*, trans. David Farrell Krell and Frank A. Capuzzi, New York, NY.: Harper & Row, pp. 59–78.

—— (1975b) *The End of Philosophy*, trans. Joan Stambaugh, London: Souvenir Press.

—— (1976a) *Gedachtes/Thoughts* [1971], trans. Keith Hoeller, *Philosophy Today* 20, pp. 286–91.

—— (1976b) 'Only a God Can Save us' [1976], trans. Maria P. Alter and John Caputo, *Philosophy Today* 20, pp. 267–85. Also reproduced in Wolin (1993), pp. 91–116.

—— (1977a) *The Question Concerning Technology*, trans. William Lovitt, New York: Harper and Row, pp. 115–54.

—— (1977b) 'Why Do I Stay in the Provinces?' [1934], trans. Thomas J. Sheehan, *Listening* 12 (1977), pp. 122–5.

—— (1982) *The Basic Problems of Phenomenology* [1975: lecture course of 1927], trans. Albert Hofstadter, rev. edn, Bloomington: Indiana University Press.

—— (1983) 'Hebel – Friend of the House' [1957], trans. Bruce V. Foltz and Michael Heim, *Contemporary German Philosophy* 3, pp. 89–101.

—— (1989) *What is Philosophy?* [1955], trans. William Kluback and Jean T. Wilde, Plymouth: Vision Press, 1989.

—— (1989a) *The Principle of Reason* [1957], trans. Reginald Lilly. Bloomington and Indianapolis: Indiana University Press.

—— (1989b) *Überlieferte Sprache und Technische Sprache* [lecture of 1962], Switzerland: Erker Verlag.

—— (1992) *Parmenides* [1982: lecture course of 1943–43], trans. André Schuwer and Richard Rojcewicz, Bloomington: Indiana University Press.

—— (1992a) *History of the Concept of Time: Prolegomena* [1979: lecture course of 1925], trans. Theodore Kisiel, Bloomington: Indiana University Press.

—— (1992b) *The Fundamental Concepts of Metaphysics: World, Finitude, Solitude* [1983: lecture course of 1929–30], trans. William McNeill and Nicholas Walker, Bloomington and Indianapolis: Indiana University Press.

—— (1993) 'Die nachgelassenen Klee-Notizen', Günter Seubold (ed.) in *Heidegger Studies* 9, pp. 5–12.

—— (1996) *Hölderlin's Hymn 'The Ister'* [1984: lecture course of 1942], trans. William McNeill and Julia Davis, Bloomington: Indiana University Press.

—— (1998) *Pathmarks* [1967], trans. Frank A. Capuzzi *et al.*, William McNeill (ed.), Cambridge: Cambridge University Press.

—— (1999) *Contributions to Philosophy (From Enowning)* [1989], trans. Parvis Emad and Kenneth Maly, Bloomington: Indiana University Press.

—— (2000a) *Elucidations of Hölderlin's Poetry* [1971], trans. Keith Hoeller, Amherst, NY: Humanity Books.

—— (2000b) *Introduction to Metaphysics* [1953], trans. Gregory Fried and Richard Polt, New Haven: Yale University Press.

Heidegger, Martin and Eugen Fink (1993) *Heraclitus Seminars* [1970], trans. Charles H. Seibert, Evanston, Ill.: Northwestern University Press.

Hines, Thomas J. (1976) *The Later Poetry of Wallace Stevens: Phenomenological Parallels with Husserl and Heidegger*, Lewisburg, Pa.: Bucknell University Press.

Hodge, Joanna (1995) *Heidegger and Ethics*, London: Routledge.

Hölderlin, Friedrich (1913–23) *Sämtliche Werke*, Norbert von Hellingrath (ed.), Friedrich Seebaß and Ludwig von Pigenot, 6 vols., Munich and Leipzig: G. Müller.

Hölderlin, Friedrich (1980) *Poems and Fragments*, bilingual edn., trans. Michael Hamburger, Cambridge: Cambridge University Press.

Holub, Robert C. (1984) *Reception Theory: A Critical Introduction*, London: Methuen.

Inwood, Michael (1999) *A Heidegger Dictionary*, Oxford: Blackwell.

Kisiel, Theodor (1995) 'Heidegger's *Gesamtausgabe*: An International Scandal of Scholarship', *Philosophy Today* 31, pp. 3–15.

Kolb, D. (1995) 'Raising Atlantis: The Later Keidegger and Contemporary Philosophy', in *From Phenomenology to Thought, Errancy, and Desire: Essays in Honor of William J. Richardson, S.J.*, Babette Babich (ed.), Dordrecht: Kluwer Academic Publishers, pp. 55–69.

Krell, David Farrell (1992) *Daimon Life: Heidegger and Life-Philosophy*, Bloomington: University of Indiana Press.

Kritzman, L. D. (1988) *Foucault, Politics, Philosophy, Culture*, New York: Routledge.

Lacoue-Labarthe, Philippe (1990) *Heidegger, Art and Politics* [1987], trans. Chris Turner, Oxford: Blackwell.

—— (1999) *Poetry as Experience* [1986], trans. Andrea Tarnowski, Stanford, CA: Stanford University Press.

Lyotard, Jean-François (1989) 'The Sublime and the Avant-Garde', in Andrew Benjamin (ed.), *The Lyotard Reader*, Oxford: Basil Blackwell, pp. 196–211.

—— (1990) *Heidegger and 'the Jews'* [1988], trans. Andreas Michel and Mark Roberts, Minneapolis, London: University of Minnesota Press.

Lysaker, John T. (1993) 'Heidegger After the Fall', *Research in Phenomenology* 23, pp. 201–11.

May, Reinhard (1996) *Heidegger's Hidden Sources*, London: Routledge.

McCarthy, Thomas (1993) *Ideals and Illusions: On Reconstruction and Deconstruction in Contemporary Critical Theory*, Cambridge Mass.: MIT Press.

McWhorter, Ladelle (ed.) (1992) *Heidegger and the Earth: Essays in Environmental Philosophy*, Kirksville, Mo.: Thomas Jefferson University Press.

Macann, Christopher (ed.) (1992) *Martin Heidegger: Critical Assessments*, 4 vols, London: Routledge.

Milchman, Alan and Alan Rosenberg (1996) *Martin Heidegger and the Holocaust*, Atlantic Heights, NJ.: Humanities Press.

Mugerauer, Robert (1988) *Heidegger's Language and Thought*, Atlantic Highlands, NJ: Humanities Press.

—— (1995) *Interpreting Environments: Tradition, Deconstruction, Hermeneutics*, Austin: University of Texas Press.

Ott, Hugo (1993) *Martin Heidegger: A Political Life*, trans. Allan Blunden, New York: Basic Books; London: HarperCollins.

Petzet, Heinrich Wiegand (1993) *Encounters and Dialogues with Martin Heidegger 1929–1976*, trans. Parvis Emad and Kenneth Maly, Chicago: University of Chicago Press.

Plimpton, George (ed.) (1967) *Writers at Work: The Paris Review Interviews*, New York, NY: Viking.

Polt, Richard (1999) *Heidegger*, London: UCL Press.

Preston, Beth (1993) 'Heidegger and Artificial Intelligence', *Philosophy and Phenomenological Research* 53, pp. 35–51.

Rapaport, Hermann (1989) *Heidegger and Derrida: Reflections on Time and Language*, Lincoln, Neb.: University of Nebraska Press.

—— (1997) *Is There Truth in Art?*, Ithaca, NY.: Cornell University Press.

Rée, Jonathan (1998) *Heidegger*, London: Phoenix.

Ricoeur, Paul (1981) *Hermeneutics and the Human Sciences*, Cambridge: Cambridge University Press.

Riddel, Joseph N. (1974) *The Inverted Bell: Modernism and the Counter-poetics of William Carlos Williams,* Baton Rouge: Louisiana State University Press.

Safranski, Rüdiger (1998) *Martin Heidegger: Between Good and Evil*, trans. Ewald Osers, Cambridge Mass.: Harvard University Press.

Sallis, John (ed.) (1993) *Reading Heidegger: Commemorations*, Bloomington: Indiana University Press.

Schirmacher, Wolfgang (1983) *Technik und Gelassenheit*, Freiburg: Alber.

Schürmann, Reiner (1990) *Heidegger on Being and Acting: From Principles to Anarchy* [1987], trans. Christine-Marie Gros, Bloomington: Indiana University Press.

Spanos, William V. (ed.) (1976) *Martin Heidegger and the Question of Literature: Towards a Postmodern Literary Hermeneutics*, Bloomington: Indiana University Press.

—— (1993) *Heidegger and Criticism: Retrieving the Cultural Politics of Destruction*, Minneapolis: University of Minnesota Press, 1993.

Spengler, Oswald (1926–29) *The Decline of the West*, trans. Charles Francis Atkinson, London: G. Allen & Unwin.

Steiner, George (1991) *Martin Heidegger*, Chicago: University of Chicago Press.

—— (1992) 'Through that Glass Darkly,' *Salmagundi* No. 93, pp. 37–50.

Stoppard, Tom (1997) *The Invention of Love*, London: Faber and Faber.

Taminiaux, Jacques (1993) 'The Origin of "The Origin of the Work of Art"', in Sallis (ed.) *Reading Heidegger: Commemorations*, Bloomington: Indiana University Press, pp. 392–404.

Vattimo, Gianni (1988) *The End of Modernity*, trans. Jon R. Snyder, Oxford: Basil Blackwell.

Wittgenstein, Ludwig (1974a) *Philosophical Investigations* [1953], trans. G. E. M. Anscombe, Oxford: Basil Blackwell.

—— (1974b) *Philosophical Grammar*, trans. A. Kenny, R. Rhees (ed.), Berkeley: University of California Press.

Wolin, Richard (ed.) (1993) *The Heidegger Controversy: A Critical Reader*, Cambridge Mass.: MIT, pp. 29–39.

Young, Julian (1997) *Heidegger, Philosophy, Nazism*, Cambridge: Cambridge University Press.

Zimmerman, Michael E. (1990) *Heidegger's Confrontation with Modernity: Technology, Politics, Art*, Bloomington: Indiana University Press.

INDEX

Saussure, Ferdinand de 142
Schank, Roger 20
Schelling, F. W. J. 51–2, 99
Schurmann, Rainer 2
science 11, 13, 21, 23, 33, 34–5,
  37, 67, 68, 142, 145, 151;
  scientific knowledge 2
scientism 21, 143
secret 118–19, 132
sexual difference 142
Shakespeare, William: *Hamlet* 44–5,
  57–8, 93–5, 107; *Henry V*,
  153
silence, Heidegger's 124–6
singularity 47–51, 58, 61, 62,
  101, 102, 129, 130, 132, 147,
  152
Sophocles 15, 32, 95, 107, 152;
  Antigone 63
Spanos, William 141, 144; *Heidegger
  and Criticism* 134
Spengler, Oswald: *The Decline of the
  West* 3
Spinoza, Baruch de 150–1
Steiner, George 126
Stevens, Wallace 143
Stoppard, Tom 15
Stravinsky, Igor 65
structuralism 143–4
sublime 64, 133
super-man 29

Taoism 84, 86
techne 48, 77
technology 30, 36, 37, 48, 64, 66,
  67, 68, 97, 124, 135, 136, 139,
  151
techno-science 34–5, 42, 68, 97,
  109, 120; techno-scientific
  civilization 10
theoreticism 13, 15, 17, 19, 20, 30,
  43, 47, 55, 72

theoria 16
theory, the theoretical 9, 11, 12,
  13, 14, 15, 16, 18, 21, 24, 37
theory of everything 35–6
tourist industry 64
trace 76–8
tradition 13, 18, 23, 27, 71, 72, 74,
  129, 140, 151
Trakl, Georg 98, 102, 104, 109,
  113, 129, 130
translation 31, 51, 73, 75–80, 81,
  88, 91; internal translation 80–1,
  84, 101, 102
truth 4, 11, 12, 13, 21–3, 29, 31,
  33, 42, 44, 49, 50, 51, 53, 59, 62,
  63, 64, 77, 84, 101, 130, 144,
  148; correspondence theory of
  truth 22–3, 44–5; *see also aletheia*

undecidability 58
understanding 9, 12, 13, 14, 17, 39,
  73, 81, 118, 147; non-theoretical
  or pre-reflective understanding
  12, 15, 16, 17, 20, 25, 146
university 63, 69, 94, 139–40, 152;
  see also academy; education,
  education system
unthought, the 31, 59, 68, 75–6,
  77, 78, 84, 86, 89, 91, 103–4,
  131

Valéry, Paul 112, 137
Van Gogh, Vincent 46, 47, 86
Vattimo, Gianni 54
Virgil 44, 107
Vogeler, Heinrich 64

Weber, Max 104
Weimar Republic 135
West (the West) 5, 6, 11, 16, 28,
  29, 38, 71, 74, 85, 86, 113, 125,
  126, 139, 140